DIGITAL HEALTH IMPLEMENTATION GUIDE FOR THE PACIFIC

MAY 2021

ASIAN DEVELOPMENT BANK

6 ADB Avenue, Mandaluyong City, 1550 Metro Manila, Philippines
Tel +63 2 632 4444; Fax +63 2 636 2444
www.adb.org

ISBN 978-92-9262-855-0 (print), 978-92-9262-856-7 (electronic); 978-92-9262-857-4 (ebook)
Publication Stock No. TIM210178-2
DOI: http://dx.doi.org/10.22617/TIM210178-2

Notes:
In this publication, "$" refers to United States dollars.
ADB recognizes "China" as the People's Republic of China
All photos by ADB.

Cover design by Karmen Karamanian.

On the cover: Digital health information systems are an important investment to provide data for informed decision-making (photo by ADB).

CONTENTS

TABLES

FIGURES

FOREWORD

This guide sets out a clear and accessible pathway for countries and those working in the health sector seeking to invest in and implement digital health. It outlines issues to be considered in maximizing the benefits and minimizing the risks of digital health development, to ensure strong beneficial impacts from investing in digital health. The guide is structured around a logical progression of activities to be undertaken at various stages of a country's digital health maturity.

The guide is aimed at two key audiences: health managers and people working in information and communication technology in the health sector. It aims to guide decision makers in thinking about the digital health investment process, and help digital health specialists to support investment decisions and their implementation.

The guide has been developed with extensive contributions from practitioners, government staff, and development partners in the Pacific health sector. It includes experiences from Pacific countries that have already invested in digital health, and brings together a collection of practical tools and resources to guide all stages of digital health implementation and use.

This is the first digital health implementation guide of the Asian Development Bank (ADB) that is specific to the Pacific region, and it builds on other ADB resources on digital health. ADB is committed to supporting the Pacific region to adopt digital technologies in the health sector to improve service quality and effectiveness. This commitment includes grants, loans, and technical assistance to help developing member countries plan, develop, and invest in digital health systems.

Leah Gutierrez

Director General
Pacific Department
Asian Development Bank

ACKNOWLEDGMENTS

This guide presents the analysis and recommendations of the Asian Development Bank (ADB) and is supported by case studies from Pacific developing member countries to strengthen its relevance. The report was financed by ADB's Regional Technical Assistance Pacific Information and Communication Technology Investment Plan and ADB's Pacific Regional Technical Assistance Developing the Health Sector. The work was carried out in 2020 and aims to inform government and development partner initiatives to strengthen digital health across the Pacific. It directly guides ADB program design and implementation of digital health investments.

The guide was prepared by Lanette Burrows, ADB consultant, with inputs and under the overall guidance from Inez Mikkelsen-Lopez, Health Specialist, ADB's Pacific Department. Susann Roth, Advisor and Chief of Knowledge Advisory Services, ADB's Sustainable Development and Climate Change Department, provided valuable insights that informed the guide's overall direction. It has further benefited from inputs provided by Peter Nicholls, ICT Specialist, ADB's Pacific Department and Michael Bainbridge, ADB consultant.

The guide also benefited from the support of Sibesh Bhattacharya, Principal Infrastructure Specialist; Kelvin Lam, Health Specialist; Cecilia Caparas, Associate Knowledge Management Officer and Raymond Vera, Senior Operations Assistant. This guide was edited by Justine Gannon, ADB consultant and layout and design was executed by Karmen Karamanian, ADB consultant.

We would also like to thank those people who contributed detailed case studies from their experiences of implementing digital health initiatives on the ground in the Pacific region.

ABBREVIATIONS

2FA	2-Factor Authentication
ADB	Asian Development Bank
AeHIN	Asia eHealth Information Network
API	Application Program Interface
ENHIS	Electronic National Health Information System (Papua New Guinea)
DIIG	(WHO) Digital Implementation Investment Guide
DSS	Decision Support Systems
EMR	Electronic Medical Record
FHIR	Fast Healthcare Interoperability Resources
IaaS	Infrastructure as a Service
ICD	International Classification of Diseases
ICT	information and communication technology
IT	information technology
ITU	International Telecommunications Union
HI	Health Informatics
HIM	Health Information Management
HIMSS	Healthcare Information and Management Systems Society, Inc.
HIS	Health Information Systems
HIT	Health Information Technology
HMN	(WHO) Health Metrics Network
IVR	Interactive Voice Response
JSON	Javascript Object Notation
LAN	local area network
LOINC	Logical Observation Identifiers Names and Codes
LOM	Lights-Out Management
MAPS	mHealth Assessment and Planning for Scale
MDM	Mobile Device Management
NDOH	National Department Of Health (Papua New Guinea)
NGO	nongovernment organization
NHID	National Health ID
OpenHIE	Open Health Information Exchange
PaaS	Platform as a Service
PACS	Picture Archiving and Communication Systems
PHI	Protected Health Information
PHIN	Pacific Health Information Network
PIMS	Patient Information Management System
PNG	Papua New Guinea
REST	Representational State Transfer
RFP	Request For Proposal
RPO	Recovery Point Objectives
RTO	Recovery Time Objectives
SaaS	Software as a Service
SILA	Standards and Interoperability Lab Asia
SOAP	Simple Object Access Protocol
TCO	Total Cost of Ownership
TOR	terms of reference
UHC	Universal Health Care
UNSW	University of New South Wales
VLAN	virtual local area networks
VPN	Virtual Private Network
WHO	World Health Organization
WHO CC	World Health Organization Collaborating Centre
XML	extensible markup language

ABOUT THIS GUIDE

Implementing digital health—inspiring, developing, and enhancing knowledge in Pacific island countries

The Digital Health Implementation Guide is a concise playbook for governments and health teams adopting information and communication technology within healthcare settings. Specifically designed for Pacific island countries, this guide is practical, easy-to-understand and can be used at any stage of a country's digital health maturity.

Universal health coverage is a primary goal for Pacific island countries. Digital technologies are becoming part of that solution. Sustainable gains in using digital technologies for healthcare can be made by strengthening leadership and governance, developing capacity, and collaborating at a regional level. This guide outlines foundational and operational aspects needed to implement digital health effectively and sustainably. Using experience-based examples, this guide is practical and realistic, with actionable goals for teams.

At the July 2019 Pacific Health Information Network (PHIN) meeting in Noumea, New Caledonia, 16 member states came together[1] to share information about digital health and plan a collective way forward. Countries acknowledged being at different stages in their digital health journey. About 60% of Pacific island countries do not yet have a digital health strategy and many have not included digital health in their health sector development plans. Most countries with a digital health road map have not yet achieved their digital health goals, stating that implementing scalable digital health solutions is challenging.

Part of the problem is navigating the available digital health resources. Much of the supporting literature is theoretical, detailed, lengthy, and difficult to use. Health officials asked PHIN for guidance on implementing digital health at a national scale. The PHIN Secretariat requested the Asian Development Bank (ADB) to draft a guide—synthesizing existing resources alongside best practices for PHIN member countries.

Pacific island countries face similar challenges in implementing digital health: hard-to-reach populations, the threat of climate change with recurrent disasters, relatively small populations, reliance on other countries for imports of information and communication technology, inadequate telecommunication infrastructure, and human resource constraints. These challenges require a digital health implementation guide specifically focused on the context for Pacific island countries.

Collaboration

The Digital Health Implementation Guide was created in collaboration with the PHIN Board, PHIN countries and the World Health Organization (WHO) Collaborating Centre at the University of New South Wales, Australia (WHO CC, UNSW). The guide synthesizes best practices and references with foundational resources, checklists, and procedures.

Practice spotlights highlight experiential learning from key experts including Robert Akers, Project Manager, PNG Health Services Sector Development Project & Rural Primary Health Service Deliver Project; Dr Siale Akauola, CEO, Ministry of Health, Tonga; Mark Landry, Regional Advisor—Health Information Systems, World Health Organization; Philip Christian Zuniga, SIL-Asia Lab Director; Pua Hunter, Director of ICT—Office of the Prime Minister, Government of the Cook Islands; Daphne Ringi, Director—Planning and Funding, Te Marae Ora—Ministry of Health; and Sheldon Yett, UNICEF Pacific Representative.

[1] Convened by the Pacific Community (SPC) and WHO.

HOW TO USE THIS GUIDE

The Digital Health Implementation Guide is a comprehensive playbook for navigating how to implement your digital health system. You can use this guide in its entirety or jump into a specific section where you need guidance and support.

A THREE-PART STRUCTURE

The guide is structured in three parts:

YELLOW
LEADERSHIP AND GOVERNANCE

BLUE
TECHNICAL

GREEN
ANALYTICS AND INFORMATION

SECTIONS

Within each part, sections are organized in a logical progression.
Each section can be viewed "at-a-glance" and can be referred to at decision-making junctures.
Sections can be used on their own or in any order.

1. Overview:
Describes the topic

2. Goals to accomplish:
Outcomes to achieve

3. Why the topic is important:
Drivers and reasons

4. Best practices:
Suggestions for success

5. Pitfalls:
What to avoid

6. Quick tips:
An idea or quick action

7. Practice spotlight:
Real-world examples from subject matter experts in the Pacific Islands or literature

8. Resources:

- *Resource:* Tools tailored for this guide.
- *Reference:* External links to information and tools.

 Denotes a gender-related topic

 Denotes an inclusivity topic

With increased internet connectivity, Pacific island countries have an opportunity to connect remote health facilities with larger health centers for greater information exchange to assist those working in health information planning, implementation, and design (photo by ADB).

LEADERSHIP AND GOVERNANCE

LEADERSHIP AND GOVERNANCE

CONTENTS

LAYING THE GROUNDWORK

1. INSTITUTIONAL READINESS

1.1 Overview

Implementing digital health systems is challenging. Digital health systems change the way people do their jobs and change the way they receive health information. Before planning or implementing digital health systems, it is important to know if an organization, institution, or even a region or country is ready to adopt new technologies and processes. It is especially important to understand how healthcare providers, patients, and program managers perceive digital health systems—positively or negatively. Measuring readiness is one of the first steps in developing a digital health strategy.

1.2 Goals to accomplish

A readiness assessment is a standard way to measure readiness and gather opinions from stakeholders. The process should include managers and healthcare providers from a variety of settings and with different experiences to gather a broad range of opinions. The following steps are recommended:

1. Review the recommended Readiness Assessment Tool and Questionnaire[2] developed and tested by the University of Calgary and their partners. The University of Calgary's assessment tool provides questions for both healthcare providers and managers; the assessment tool is easy to understand and in a small number of questions, covers the most important aspects of a digital health assessment.
2. Identify diverse individuals from across the government and organizations to participate in the assessment to gather opinions from all types of users from both urban and rural settings.
3. Undertake semi-structured interviews with stakeholders in person or via phone, or hold a workshop to complete the Readiness Assessment Tool and Questionnaire.
4. Compile the scores, comments, opinions, and suggestions to use as inputs to developing a digital health strategy.

1.3 Importance

Why readiness assessments are important

The readiness assessment should uncover any potential challenges that may impede successfully implementing a digital health strategy. The readiness assessment should also help uncover ways to mitigate risks and improve the successful adoption of digital health technologies. The earlier issues are identified, the easier they are to address during planning and implementation.

1.4 Best practices

Identify the right readiness topics and questions

Carefully review the topics and questions in the readiness questionnaire. Ensure they are appropriate to your audience, geography, and environment. Form a working group, including those writing the digital health strategy and running the implementation, to review the questions, identify stakeholders, and undertake the assessment.[2] The key components of a digital health readiness assessment are:

- **Core readiness**—technology needs and the level of comfort and trust with that technology
- **Technological readiness**—the physical access to technology and the availability and affordability of technologies
- **Learning readiness**—availability of programs and resources for training healthcare providers
- Societal readiness—sociocultural factors, gender issues and interaction between institutions and organizations

2 Khoja, S., et.al. 2007. e-Health Readiness Assessment Tools for Healthcare Institutions in Developing Countries. *Telemedicine Journal and e-Health*. September.

Define terms or ideas

Some stakeholders may not be familiar with digital health concepts or systems. To encourage consistency in use of technology terms and ideas, provide clear definitions for interviewers or workshop participants. Consider using the Digital Health Terminology Guide published by the Asian Development Bank (ADB) and the Asian eHealth Information Network.[3] This guide is a comprehensive and well-organized reference with excellent visuals for easier comprehension of concepts.

Include strategic branches of government

In addition to the Ministry of Health, other branches of government will be directly or indirectly involved with implementing digital health systems. These stakeholders must be involved in the readiness assessment. Running a convergence workshop at the readiness stage,[4] where government departments can identify strengths and weaknesses, will kick-start the development of a national digital strategy. This early involvement helps to create a shared vision and cooperation. If the branches of government listed here do not exactly match your country, include representatives from an equivalent department in your readiness assessment:

- **Ministry of Health**—typically the custodian of digital health projects
- **Ministry of Infrastructure, Science and Technology, and Ministry of Transport and Communications**—responsible for communications and infrastructure and providing a platform to support the digital health technology
- **Ministry of Education and Skills Development**—ensures that technical literacy issues are addressed so end users are digital health ready
- **Ministry for Women**—ensures that women and women's issues are included in digital health initiatives
- **Ministry of Justice**—responsible for administering law and ensuring relevant laws and policies are in place for e-initiatives and data protection
- **Ministry of Finance and Development Planning**—ensures finances are available for digital health implementation and manages the budget
- **Ministry of Interior**—responsible for national identification, birth and death reporting.

Include stakeholders from outside the government

The relationships between different stakeholders form a complex web that must be understood and managed.[5] Take a holistic and comprehensive approach to assessing digital health readiness, where possible. It is important to include stakeholders from outside the government such as the private sector, state-owned enterprises, statutory corporations, international agencies, and international partnerships. They will have valuable input to the readiness assessment.

1.5 Pitfalls

Don't ignore social structures

Depending on your country or region, rooted social structures can impact how you engage stakeholders in the readiness assessment. For example, in some communities, there is a cultural protocol of consulting chiefs, or village or community leaders. Conversely, in some communities, proactive engagement may be required to ensure sufficient consultation with women and women's groups. It is important that these considerations are given sufficient priority in digital health readiness assessments (refer to footnote 2). For these stakeholders, a separate digital health readiness tool may need to be developed to solicit appropriate community-level input.

Do not skip the readiness assessment step

The government, your organization or the community may feel that it is ready to adopt technology, especially if some digital health tools, such as mobile phones, are already in use. But adopting technology will disrupt and change healthcare processes and could impact patient care. It is important to perform a readiness assessment, even in a small way.

3 ADB and Asian eHealth Information Network. 2018. *Digital Health Terminology Guide*. March. http://sil-asia.org/digital-health-terminology-guide/.

4 Roth, S., Parry, J., and Thit, W.M. 2018. *Digital Health Convergence Meeting Tool Kit*. November. https://www.adb.org/publications/digital-health-convergence-meeting-tool-kit.

5 Marcelo, A., Medeiros, D., Ramesh, K., Roth, S., and Wyatt, P. 2018. *Transforming Health Systems Through Good Digital Health Governance*. ADB. February. https://www.adb.org/sites/default/files/publication/401976/sdwp-051-transforming-health-systems.pdf.

1.6 Quick tip

During stakeholder interviews, make sure everyone is using the same set of questions with the definitions for technology and other terminology explicitly defined. Try not to let the interviewees take the conversation too far away from the set questions.

1.7 Practice spotlight

Institutional readiness in Papua New Guinea—mobile data collection and reporting[6]

A readiness assessment was undertaken in 2017 to understand the successes and gaps of Papua New Guinea's (PNG) Rural Primary Health Services Delivery Project overseen by the National Department of Health (NDOH). The project aimed to strengthen the legacy electronic National Health Information System (eNHIS) with an interoperable mobile phone solution for data transmission and reporting.

The technology was introduced into five provinces between 2014 and 2017—West New Britain, Milne Bay, Enga, Bougainville and Western Highlands—with the 2017 assessment evaluating the project midway to identify achievements and uncover gaps and risks to be addressed for the project to be successfully and sustainably implemented to 184 facilities across 22 provinces.

The assessment examined the expected deliverables at the midpoint of the project and verified that the pilot solution was ready for a nationwide rollout. Questions posed by the assessment were:

- Is the system capable of meeting the NDOH's needs at the provincial level?
- Is the system capable of meeting stakeholders' information needs for health service planning, management and reporting?
- Are healthcare workers ready and able to implement the system?

Findings of the assessment showed that eNHIS was successfully introduced into five pilot provinces in facilities with existing paper-based NHIS systems. Findings also showed that the eNHIS established a significant and positive change in data collection, quality, timeliness, and data use. Health workers were enthusiastic about the system, especially at the facility and provincial level.

However, the assessment also found considerable challenges arising from the PNG health system itself, including effective use of data by decision makers, as well as the need for increased oversight by the NDOH in governance, thought leadership, and contract management of the project.

The assessment showed that if the identified risks were addressed and mitigated, rolling out to the remaining 17 provinces should proceed.

1.8 Resources and references

Are you ready?

Resource: Use the Readiness Assessment Tool and Questionnaire to undertake surveys and run workshops to gather information to determine readiness to implement digital health.

Reference: Use the Digital Health Terminology Guide for consistent comprehension of concepts.

Reference: Use the ADB AeHIN Convergence Workshop Toolkit as a framework for planning workshops.

6 Matheson, D., Douglas, M., Bhattacharya, S., 2017. *Independent Review of the PNG NHIS for Rural Primary Health Services Delivery.* Manila: ADB.

2. SYSTEM ASSESSMENT AND DIGITAL MATURITY

2.1 Overview

A shared understanding of the 'as-is' state of healthcare technology will inform the development of a digital health strategy. Assessing existing systems and digital maturity will help to identify what is currently available and where improvement is needed. This assessment will review how health-related information is collected and flows through the system. It will also help to gain an understanding of the environment digital health systems are being implemented in or will be implemented in the future. A well-crafted assessment framework will investigate technology products, data sources, data management, human resources and information dissemination and use.[7] The first digital health assessment should act as a baseline. Then, periodic assessments can track how the maturity has changed and where further adjustments or new implementations are needed.

2.2 Goals to accomplish

Collect data through workshops such as a convergence workshop where ideas are gathered and stakeholders form a common understanding of the problems and goals (refer to footnote 4). Data can also be collected through stakeholder interviews and questionnaires about the state of existing digital health systems. The results of the assessment and maturity review become inputs to the national digital health strategy, which provides a vision and guidelines for a future state.

2.3 Importance

Why system assessments and digital maturity are important

Without a baseline of the current digital health systems, it is difficult to precisely determine the gaps and plan the next steps to strengthen those digital health information systems.

Undertaking a digital health information system assessment is a necessary step toward building a strong, country-level digital health information system.

2.4 Best practices

Use a framework to guide the selection of assessment criteria

Defining the evaluation criteria for a national digital health information system can be difficult (refer to footnote 7). To help guide the selection of topics and questions, use the Global Digital Health Index, one of the WHO-recommended digital maturity models. A structured approach will help data collection and analysis, which will be used as inputs to developing a digital health strategy.

Involve stakeholders with different roles and responsibilities across healthcare

Invite stakeholders from both national and subnational levels, at management and healthcare levels, to participate in the assessment. Diversity across stakeholders is critical to ensure no groups are underrepresented. These participants may include representatives from central statistics office, ministry of health, other ministries, public health institutions, universities, donors, United Nations organizations, nongovernment organizations (NGOs), private health professional associations, and faith-based health providers (refer to footnote 7).

[7] World Health Organization (WHO). 2008. *Assessing the National Health Information System, An Assessment Tool.* Version 4.00. Health Metrics Network.

Look at all data sources

Data collected though health information systems is used at various levels for decision-making. For example, information on patient records, care needs, and available treatment is used for clinical decision-making. Health facility data such as drug procurement records, equipment and supplies, and aggregate patient health data is used for facility and operations management. Population data such as census; vital statistics, including births and deaths; and household surveys are used to prioritize service needs. Disease surveillance is used to identify and track epidemic and disease control. Patient-level, health facility, population, and public health surveillance data are all important to build a comprehensive view of a national system and evaluating all data sources should be included in the digital health information system assessment.[8]

Identify a champion

Leadership and coordination are needed to organize the assessment activities and collect, collate, and analyze the data required. Having a champion is essential for the success of the assessment. The champion could be from the Ministry of Health or possibly the National Statistics Office or from a large healthcare program within the country. The champion should help to articulate the objectives, ensure that the steps of the assessment continue as planned, and communicate findings to stakeholders.

2.5 Pitfalls

Clearly define the scope of the digital health assessment

Expectations that a digital health assessment will evaluate every system to a high level of detail may lead to disappointment for management and ministries. Because digital health systems are complex, it is important to detail the scope of the assessment as part of planning, before the evaluation starts. The scope boundaries should include the systems, hardware and software, departments, users, and stakeholders to be evaluated. Alignment to core indicators that are routinely reported will ensure the availability of data. Breaking up the evaluation into smaller segments and tailoring questions to those segments is also helpful to limit the scope.[9]

Clearly articulate the intention of the assessment

Stakeholders will have differing opinions about the use or implementation of digital health technologies; determining the areas to assess and the questions to ask can be very challenging. Having a common national vision for the overall functions and end-user impact of a digital health system will help coordinate and solidify the intention of the digital health assessment. Clearly articulate the reason for the assessment and how the information will inform decision-making. This articulation will help to guide your choice of evaluation questions. The evaluation criteria topics and scoring system should be defined up front.

Select the right participants

Some stakeholders may be reluctant to participate in a digital health assessment. The process takes time away from regular duties and answering questions, if done well, takes a lot of thought and effort.  It may be difficult to find enough of the right, qualified representatives to participate. To increase the coverage of participants, encourage and motivate management to get involved and outline opportunities for organizational improvement and learning.

2.6 Quick tip

Organize the evaluation questions and scoring into a spreadsheet so that you can easily compile the results and display them in summary tables and graphs.

[8] WHO. 2008. *Toolkit on monitoring health systems strengthening, Health Information Systems,* June.

[9] Ammenwerth, E., Gräber, S., Herrmann G., Bürkled, T., König., J. 2003. Evaluation of health information systems—problems and challenges. *International Journal of Medical Informatics* July.

2.7 Practice spotlight

Health Information Systems in the Pacific—at a glance[10]

In 2016, the status of Pacific island countries' health information systems (HIS) was assessed to identify challenges and opportunities for strengthening these systems.

Fifteen of the 21 Pacific island countries that participated in the assessment had completed the HIS Hub Rapid Assessment, developed by The University of Queensland. Eight digital health areas were assessed: HIS resources, financial and human resources, infrastructure, indicators, data sources, data management, data quality, and dissemination and use.

Some 116 challenges were identified and broadly categorized into: people (40); processes (29); technology (25); and other challenges (22).

The most significant challenges were shortages in human resources, financial resources, and human resource capacity. Developing HIS policies and legislation also needed strengthening. The data was aggregated and detailed by country.

The same assessment was previously undertaken in 2013 and six countries were able to compare their results:

> *"Six indicators appear to present a constant challenge for the six countries: HIS policy, trained staff, budget items, data dictionary, data management procedures, and metadata."*

Overall, the six countries showed continued investment in HIS systems and four countries showed improvement between 2013 and 2016.

2.8 Resources and references

What's your baseline?

Without a baseline of the current digital health systems, it is hard to identify the gaps in your digital health system and plan how to strengthen those systems. A digital health information system assessment is a necessary step toward building a strong, country-level digital health platform.

The WHO Health Metrics Network (HMN) tool developed by the HMN (now closed), helps countries identify strengths and gaps in national resources, policies, data sources, management, and quality. The HMN tool focuses on two core requirements of health system strengthening: enhancing the entire health information and statistical systems and concentrating efforts on strengthening country leadership for health information production and use.

Reference: A detailed step-by-step guide for using the WHO Health Metrics Network tool (HMN tool)

Resource: An interactive spreadsheet workbook. An assessment framework is established with score selection in a series of tabs. The Summary tab provides a summary score sheet. The framework and the questions can be adjusted for your country or institution context. (HMN tool) Health Metrics Network tool V4.00

Reference: Digital maturity model: Global Digital Health Index

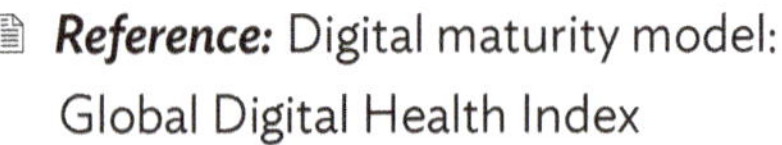

---

[10] WHO. 2017. *Health information systems in the Pacific—at a glance 2016*. Regional Office for the Western Pacific. Manila, Philippines. https://apps.who.int/iris/rest/bitstreams/1147902/retrieve.

POLICIES AND STRATEGIES

3. DIGITAL HEALTH STRATEGY

"A national eHealth strategy serves as an umbrella for planning and coordinating different national eHealth efforts while considering fundamental elements in terms of regulatory, governance, standards, human capacity, financing, and policy contexts."[11] *WHO*

3.1 Overview

Implementing digital health and ICT in healthcare is difficult and requires significant human resources and financial investment.[12] A digital health strategy is essential to describe the requirements of any system that is put in place, to provide evidence-based guidance for developing the systems, and to justify expenditure. A digital health strategy is not necessarily a stand-alone document; it can be integrated into the national health strategy. A digital health strategy should be clear about its objectives and assess factors of inequality, aiming to leverage the potential of digital health technologies to promote equity in health and not widen disparities.

3.2 Goals to accomplish

A digital health strategy should outline:

- what will be achieved
- who will benefit
- who needs to be involved
- how resources should be allocated.

A sustainable digital health solution is best designed and developed organically with stakeholders to addresses the needs of a specific healthcare system at a facility, regional, or national level. A successful digital health strategy should be simple and not include detailed plans or architectures; it should be a functional and guiding document that all stakeholders refer to and agree to.

3.3 Importance

Why is a digital health strategy important?

Implementing technology at a national scale is extremely complex and costly, often taking longer and requiring more resources than anticipated. Many systems simply fail outright[13] or are not sustainable, especially in limited-resource settings. Because funding may be scarce, a digital health strategy is essential for evidence-based guidance, describing needs and justifying expenditure to ensure investments are used to increase 'value', such as increasing patient load capacity, reducing adverse drug reactions or any other outcome important to the healthcare delivery system.

11 Krishnamurthy, R. 2015. Developing a National eHealth Strategy. *World Health Organization Headquarters Ministry of Public Health Conference on eHealth Strategy*. Bangkok, Thailand. 18 March.

12 Scott, R.E. and Mars, M. 2013. Principles and Framework for eHealth Strategy Development. *Journal of Medical Internet Research*. Vol. 15, No 7. www.jmir.org/2013/7/e155/.

13 Granja, C., Janssen, W., Johansen, M. A. 2018. Factors Determining the Success and Failure of eHealth Interventions: Systematic Review of the Literature. *Journal of Medical Internet Research*. May. 20(5): e10235. https://www.ncbi.nlm.nih.gov/pmc/articles/PMC5954232/.

Table 1. Why do digital health implementation fail?

Reasons for adoption failure	Include in your digital health strategy
Benefits for users are not experienced quickly	Provide a road map with milestones and communicate out to users about the timing of deliverables and expected benefits
Shortage of financial resources to support implementation and organizational changes	Include a cost containment strategy, with a clear definition of how the digital health intervention will facilitate the provision of care services
Negative impact on quality of care	Include a training plan to minimize impact of new technologies on patient services
Expectation that digital health intervention should/must fit pre-established workflows	Include clinicians in the digital health strategy process to assess impact on patient service workflow
Patient privacy and security concerns	Include data security and access as a key pillar in your digital health strategy and verify that policies are implemented accordingly in each system component

3.4 Best practice

Principles and Framework for eHealth Strategy Development (refer to footnote 12) recommends seven guiding principles for successfully developing a digital health strategy. The WHO-ITU toolkit[14] also incorporates these ideas and may be useful for guiding your organization to development of a digital health strategy.

- **Include the right stakeholders:** Involve stakeholders who have the most intimate knowledge of the setting and context the digital health system will be implemented in—facility, regional, or national level. Clinicians will know how digital technologies can impact existing workflows and may be concerned about the possible negative impact of technology. But they may be concerned about the negative impact of technology. Involving stakeholders like clinicians will help gain needed buy-in for digital health strategies that will, inevitably, require time and effort to gain the proposed benefits.
- **Understand healthcare needs:** Understand the most pressing public health and healthcare services needs and align the strategy to address these needs across different segments of the population. Specifically, ensure that the healthcare needs of underrepresented populations, including women and minorities, are well understood.
- **Spread infrastructure costs**: Spread and share the cost of ICT networking infrastructure costs, such as reliable electricity, fiber-optic internet lines, cell towers, internet routers, and wireless spectrum between government, business, agriculture, education, and health sectors.
- **Develop, adapt or adopt digital health assets**: Include a wide range of technology-driven components, such as health informatics (electronic records, surveillance); telehealth (teleconsultation, social networking); e-learning (online training); and e-commerce (payment, reimbursement). Striking a balance on the focus and funding across digital health areas allows for a more sustainable and comprehensive solution and, where possible, reuse adapted or adopted technology rather than develop it from scratch.
- **Select technology that is right for the setting:** Match the needs and sophistication of the users as well be sensitive to the culture of the organization or country. Technology should be simple to adopt and should be sustainable to operate and maintain with available human and financial resources.
- **Articulate a clear and enduring vision**: Have a long-term focus and be supported by a diverse set of stakeholders.
- **Make goals specific**: Articulate specific and actionable goals, with realistic timelines.

[14] WHO-ITU. 2012. *National eHealth Strategy Toolkit*. www.itu.int/dms_pub/itu-d/opb/str/D-STR-E_HEALTH.05-2012-PDF-E.pdf.

3.5 Pitfalls

Include all stakeholders

Digital health strategies are typically developed at the national level. In addition to national visionaries, include stakeholders who perform different roles throughout the healthcare system including at the community and patient level, and avoid the serious error of the strategy development being driven by development partners.

Update your digital health strategy regularly

As part of your digital health strategy, put into place indicators that track and assess the results of implementing your digital health action plan. Critically reviewing these indicators along with adjusting the national digital health strategy as needed, should be done annually with a major update at least every 5 years.

3.6 Quick tip

Break up your Digital Health Strategy into small, manageable chunks

Developing a digital health strategy is a significant undertaking. To simplify the task, split up the work into short iterations with demonstrable output, starting with the area that has the highest importance for writing the document.

Ready. Set. Sprint!

Once the sections of the digital health strategy are agreed, set 2- or 4-week 'sprints' for writing and reviewing each section. Come together as a team to review content and remove impediments for forward progress.

3.7 Practice spotlight

The Republic of Vanuatu's Digital Health Strategy

In 2019, the Republic of Vanuatu published a 3-year digital strategy with the objective of moving the country's digital health vision,

> ***'To use sustainable, cost-effective technology, systems and processes to ensure that the right information is available to the right people at the right time to support evidence-based decision-making for managerial, planning and clinical decisions.'***[15]

Vanuatu is on the cusp of providing integrated digital health services. The country uses DHIS2 for aggregated health reporting and mSupply for pharmacy supply management and supply chain logistics. Vanuatu has a dedicated and motivated health information management staff. Their readiness to move to the next step of digital integration is high, with a strong and increasing commitment to use data for evidence-based decision-making. Furthermore, a digital health governance structure is already in place. With good commercial communications infrastructure that covers much of the country and a single health provider, the country is set to begin building a digital health system to support and strengthen their healthcare system.

The focus of Vanuatu's Digital Health Strategy is to provide simple yet instructive guidance on how to establish a digital health system that is sustainable and practical with the available human and funding resources. Currently, district level health data is being collected. The next step is to be able to incorporate operational IT systems such as electronic medical records, automatic routine data capture, and indicator calculations.

Key stakeholders acknowledge that it is not only technical capacity, but also human and organizational capacity, supported by strong management commitment and good governance, which will lead to enhancing and strengthening digital health systems in the next 3 years.

[15] Vanuatu Digital Health Strategy: Information for Action 2019–2021.

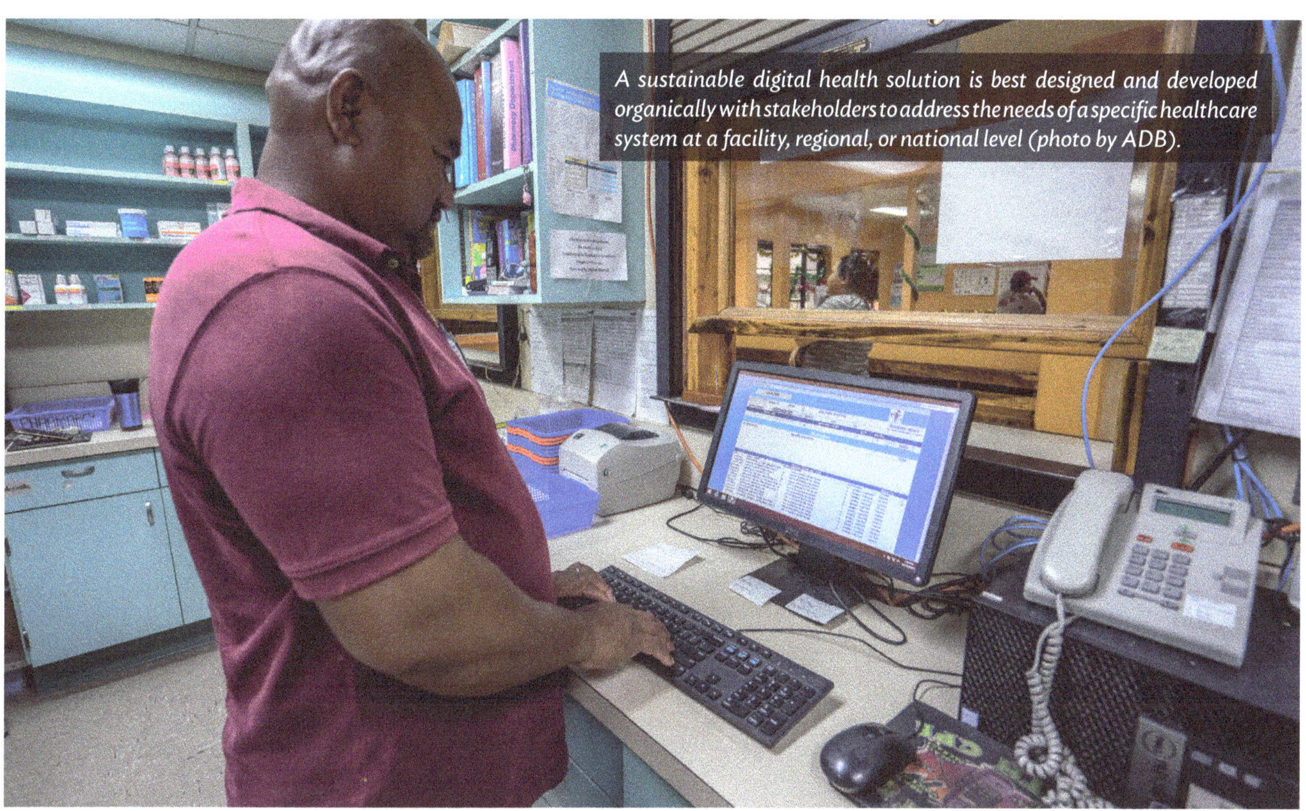

A sustainable digital health solution is best designed and developed organically with stakeholders to address the needs of a specific healthcare system at a facility, regional, or national level (photo by ADB).

3.8 Resources and references

Keep your strategy simple

A successful digital health strategy should be simple and should not include detailed plans or architectures—it should be a functional document that acts as a guide for all stakeholders to agree to and refer to.

Resource: The Digital Health Strategy Template is a simple outline for a digital health strategy that sets out what you should consider in terms of preparation, a vision and monitoring and evaluation when developing your digital health strategy.

Reference: WHO-ITU National eHealth Strategy Toolkit

Reference: Principles and Framework for eHealth Strategy Development

Reference: WHO Digital implementation investment guide (DIIG): integrating digital interventions into health programs

4. GOVERNANCE AND POLICIES

4.1 Overview

> *"Directing and coordinating eHealth development, achieving consensus on policy, protecting individuals and groups, and assuring oversight and accountability in the various aspects relating to use of information and communication technologies (ICT) for health are all part of an eHealth governance function at the national level."*[16] WHO

Clear and effective governance is critical to the success of any digital health initiative, especially national digital health strategies, which are complex and involve many stakeholders.

Establishing a well-organized and active digital health governance framework is important to ensuring that human and financial resources are optimized and that policies and legislature are aligned with national requirements.

Five key components needed to establish a governance framework and charter are as follows:[17]

1. Set an organizational framework and structure for governance of the digital health system
2. Establish a purpose for an overseeing committee and subcommittees
3. Define roles for an overseeing committee and subcommittees
4. Establish membership and membership rules
5. Define meeting frequencies.

Table 2. Key attributes when establishing a governance structure

When establishing a governance structure, these key attributes should be considered:[18]

Attribute	Apply within your governance structure
Transparency	Define, agree and document roles and responsibilities of each committee and subcommittee. Identify any conflicts of interest and remove them. Document and distribute decisions made to all stakeholders.
Leadership	Ministers and senior executives agree on policies and initiatives and champion them, demonstrating a shared commitment to the governance process.
Accountability	Senior executive officers and other leadership positions must have adequate authority and time to dedicate to digital health initiatives. Individuals must understand they are accountable for implementing tasks and initiatives.
Efficiency	There is little duplication of work areas.
Responsiveness	Committees and subcommittees must be proactive and escalate issues to minimize risk or project failure.
Diversity & inclusion	Commit to a governance structure that celebrates diversity and ensures diversity within its own structure. Ensure inclusion by establishing processes and practices that make all members welcome and provide opportunities for everyone to connect and contribute.

16 WHO. *eHealth Governance.* www.who.int/ehealth/governance/en/.

17 Health Care IT Advisor Advisory Board. *IT Governance Charter Toolkit, Implementation Resource, 2018*

18 Cabinet Implementation Unit Toolkit, Governance, Australian Government, Department of the Prime Minister and Cabinet, June 2013, www.pmc.gov.au/sites/default/files/files/pmc/implementation-toolkit-2-governance.pdf.

4.2 Goals to accomplish

Establish a digital health governance structure to establish the digital health strategy vision and guide its implementation.

4.3 Importance

Why digital health governance is important

For successful implementation of national or complex digital health strategies, a well-functioning governance structure is key.

> *"In the absence of clear governance structures, policies, processes and roles and responsibilities are blurred, resulting in fragmentation, wastage of resources, duplication of efforts, nonstrategic investment decisions, and a lack of common standards."*[19]

Without effective oversight, the return on investment for digital health initiatives is likely to be low (refer to footnote 17).

4.4 Best practices

Document and publish your organization's governance framework

A well-documented governance operating framework will help committees and subcommittees know their areas of responsibility and accountability, and help establish their boundaries. Publishing the framework creates a shared understanding of how the governance model works.

Build a culture of collaboration

Leadership promotes collaboration with shared goals, trust, open communication and strong relationships. A collaborative culture should value ethical behavior, honesty, mutual respect and collective responsibility.[20]

Separate governance from management

Governance involves strategic planning, evaluation, directing, and monitoring the digital health strategy and implementation for your organization. Governing bodies make decisions about the direction of the organization.[21] Management involves planning, building, running and monitoring the daily activities. Some of the committees in your governance framework may be responsible for overseeing these daily activities or projects; some people involved in implementing projects may also sit on the committees. However, committees should not be directly involved with day-to-day matters or implementing or running a digital health system. They should provide or develop overarching digital health guidelines and policies.

4.5 Pitfalls (refer to footnote 18)

Inadequate governance framework

Take the time to work through the steps for establishing a sound governance structure that will be able to guide and have the authority to make decisions within your organization. Doing the up-front work for identifying the committees and subcommittees, roles and responsibilities and identifying the most appropriate individuals to participate will, ultimately, save time and avoid confusion. Make adjustments as you go if the initial set up is not working effectively.

Lack of support for the governance arrangements

Senior executives and government ministers should be involved with establishing the governance structure and should support decision-making and communication processes. Public expressions of support are encouraged. Decision-making outside the governance process for national initiatives will erode participant and stakeholder commitment and lead to a lack of trust and a failure of oversight.

Unclear accountability for cross-portfolio initiatives

Many digital health initiatives cross government agencies and require shared objectives, resources and possibly reporting structures. Successful implementations of digital health initiatives depend on departments and agencies establishing shared objectives and productive working relationships for successful outcomes. Identifying who is responsible for tasks and working as a team will increase the probability of success, particularly for larger, complex initiatives.

---

19 Marcelo, A., Medeiros, D., Ramesh, K., Roth, S. and Wyatt, P. 2018. *Transforming Health Systems Through Good Digital Health Governance.* ADB Sustainable Development Working Papers Series. No. 51. February.

20 Baret, S., Sandford. N., Hida, E., Vazirani, J., Hatfield, S. 2013. *Developing an effective governance operating model. Deloitte Development LLC.*

21 Reciprocity Labs. *Guide to COBIT Best Practices.* https://reciprocitylabs.com/guide-to-cobit-best-practices/.

4.6 Quick tip

Start small

Setting up a governance structure is not easy. Start small and buildout the structure over time. With each expansion, make sure roles and responsibilities are clear and groups are held accountable for the work assigned.

4.7 Practice spotlight

ICT and the Papua New Guinea National Health Plan (2011–2020)

The PNG National Health Plan (2011–2020) specifies under Key Result Area 3 and Objective 3.4 recommends:

> *"The health sector proactively identifies and uses innovative and evolving ICT solutions and delivers accurate and timely information for planning and decision-making."*

To facilitate this national objective, the NDOH developed a digital health strategy, which outlines the vision, strategic plan, activities, and budget for the health sector. To lead this initiative, a National eHealth Steering Committee was established. The committee's responsibility was to develop a national eHealth strategic framework and bring together a broad range of stakeholders, from both the health and ICT sectors. The committee's role includes leading the development and coordination of the National eHealth Framework and oversight of national health information projects in the country. The decisions made by this committee will have significant and long-lasting impact on the hardware and software technologies selected, and on the systems selected for operations and patient-level data collection.

Following best practices, the NDOH, wrote a terms of reference for the National eHealth Steering Committee and its related Technical Working Group subcommittee. These documents were key to defining and communicating the details of each group's purpose and oversight roles. The terms of reference also identified the role of the individual group members and frequency of meetings. The Technical Working Group supports the National eHealth Steering Committee by providing expert technical advice on current and future implementations of eHealth initiatives in the country. In addition to technical support, the sub-committee also sets clinical direction for the implementation of eHealth technologies in a clinical setting. When the Secretariat, responsible for the Monitoring and Evaluation Branch of the NDOH, endorses the committee structure and strategy, it will become policy and will be available for review by citizens on the NDOH website.

By following best practices, the established committees include knowledgeable individuals who are invested in the process and understand their role and expected contribution. Having a framework in place has helped communication with stakeholders and with different departments within the government, and with donors.

There is a lot to do in PNG, but we are on the right path toward providing innovative technology solutions that will improve healthcare provision in the country.

Robert Akers—Project Manager
PNG Health Services Sector Development Project & Rural Primary Health Service Deliver Project

4.8 Resources and references

Resource: Defining and implementing a governance framework

Resource: Integrating governance questionnaire

PREPARING FOR ACTION

5. FINANCIAL MANAGEMENT

5.1 Overview

Financial management includes costing, budgeting, financing and optimizing funds to cover new digital health initiatives as well as sustaining and enhancing existing work across the portfolio. Almost half the health-related IT projects in low- and middle-income countries rely on donor funding. There is an expectation that system supports such as software licenses, hardware (cloud) services, and skilled human resources will transition to the receiving institution and be sustained going forward.[22] A robust cost management plan that looks across the portfolio of health-related IT projects, coupled with a procurement management plan will help prioritize available funding and contract vendors who can help to manage and enhance the HIS.

5.2 Goals to accomplish

Together with a digital health strategy, financial management should align priorities and budgets with available funds to build a sustainable digital health system. Because financial resources are limited, a portfolio management approach that optimizes project value will help decision makers know where to invest funds. The return on investment is in direct proportion to the preparation, process and people power allocated to each initiative.[23]

5.3 Importance

Why financial management is important

The sustainability of a digital health system and its return on investment require finances to be strategically allocated. Building and sustaining a digital health system is expensive and many IT implementations fail.[24] Following a financial management plan is a necessary step for long-term success.

5.4 Best practices

5.4.1 Create a cost management plan

Cost planning should be included as part of an organization's budgeting and planning activities. Spending should be monitored regularly and compared to the expected cost baseline.[25]

The following steps are recommended to create a strong cost management plan:[26]

- **Plan:** define how project costs will be estimated, budgeted, managed, monitored, and controlled.
- **Estimate:** determine the funds needed to complete project work.
- **Budget:** aggregate the estimated costs of individual activities to establish an authorized cost baseline.
- **Controls:** monitor the status of activities to update project costs and manage changes to the cost baseline.

5.4.2 Make informed investment decisions

Governments need to make a strong case for, what can be, large capital investments in digital health and supporting technology. Decisions should be based on input from a variety of stakeholders to optimize net socioeconomic return on investment and affordability (refer to footnote 26). Well-informed investment decisions require weighting projects and within each project, weighting technology and implementation options. Using a digital health impact framework will help organize all inputs and outputs so that a strong cost–benefit analysis is produced, making decisions easier to justify.[27]

---

22 Fritz, F., Tilahun, B, Dugas, M. 2015. Success criteria for electronic medical record implementations in low-resource settings: a systematic review. *Journal of the American Medical Informatics Association*. Volume 22, Issue 2, March.

23 Kenney, A. 2006. *A Best Practices Approach to Buying Enterprise Software, Consumer Goods Technology. August.*

24 The Standish Group International Inc. 2014. *Chaos report: 21st Anniversary Edition.*

25 Project Management Institute. 2017. *A Guide to the project management body of knowledge (PMBOK GUIDE), sixth edition.*

26 ADB. 2018. *Guidance for Investing in Digital Health, May.* www.adb.org/publications/guidance-investing-digital-health.

27 ADB. 2018. *Digital Health Impact Framework User Manual. November.* www.adb.org/sites/default/files/publication/465611/sdwp-057-digital-health-impact-framework-manual.pdf.

Figure 1. Steps for creating a strong cost management plan

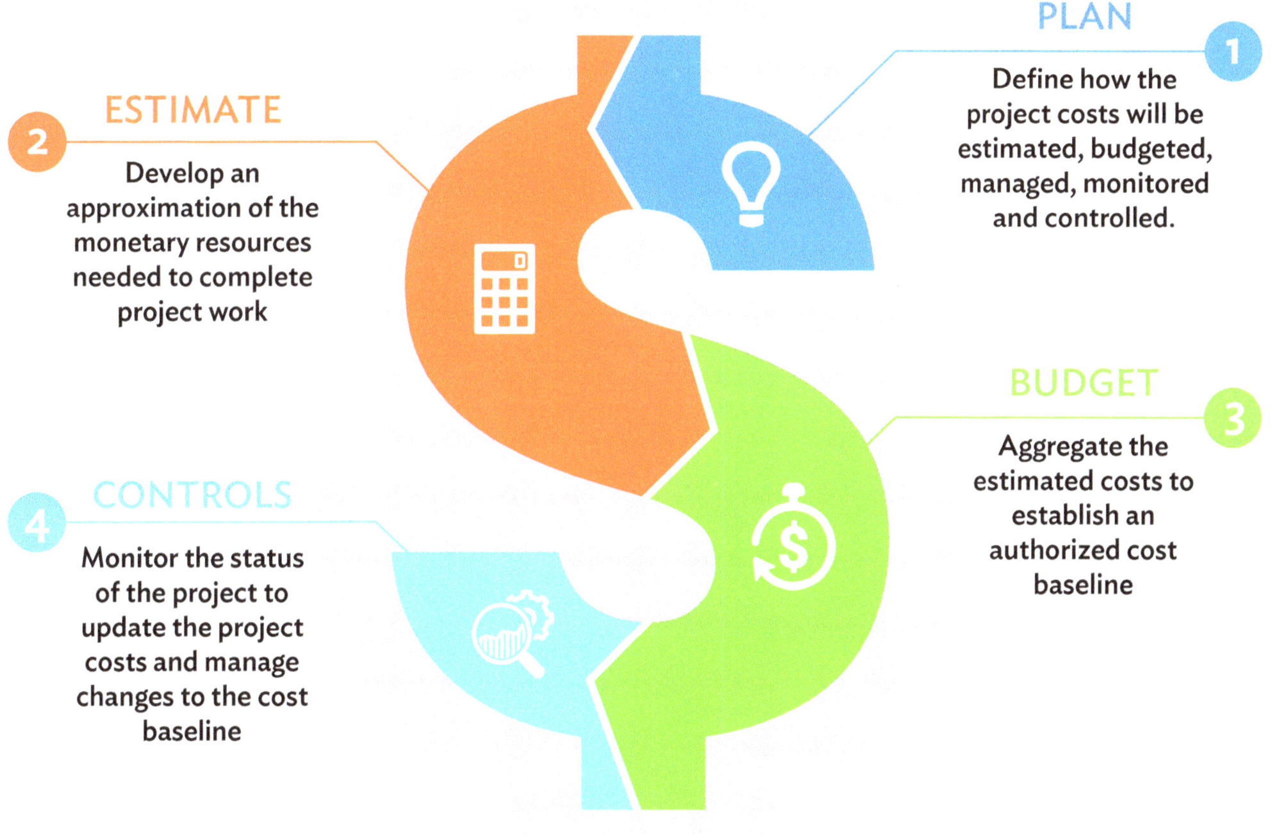
STEPS FOR
CREATING A STRONG
COST MANAGEMENT PLAN
PLAN
1
Define how the project costs will be estimated, budgeted, managed, monitored and controlled.
ESTIMATE
2
Develop an approximation of the monetary resources needed to complete project work
BUDGET
3
Aggregate the estimated costs to establish an authorized cost baseline
CONTROLS
4
Monitor the status of the project to update the project costs and manage changes to the cost baseline

5.4.3 *Calculate the Total Cost of Ownership*

When evaluating digital health system costs, it is important to assess the Total Cost of Ownership (TCO).

> *"TCO is the full assessment of information technology and services cost over time."*[28]

TCO includes both short-term and long-term costs, and direct and indirect costs. The TCO should estimate the 'real' cost of ownership, which often includes overlooked expenses such as the cost of technology adoption, implementation, loss of revenue due to a temporary loss of productivity during implementation. Revenue reductions should also be taken into account for example fewer redundancies, fewer errors and shorter lengths of hospital stays or fewer patient visits.[29]

[28] Green, J. 2019. How much EHR costs and how to set your budget. *EHR in Practice, March.*

[29] Menachemi, N. and Collum, T. 2011. Benefits and drawbacks of electronic health record systems. *Risk Management and Healthcare Policy. 2011.*

Figure 2. Steps for creating a procurement management plan

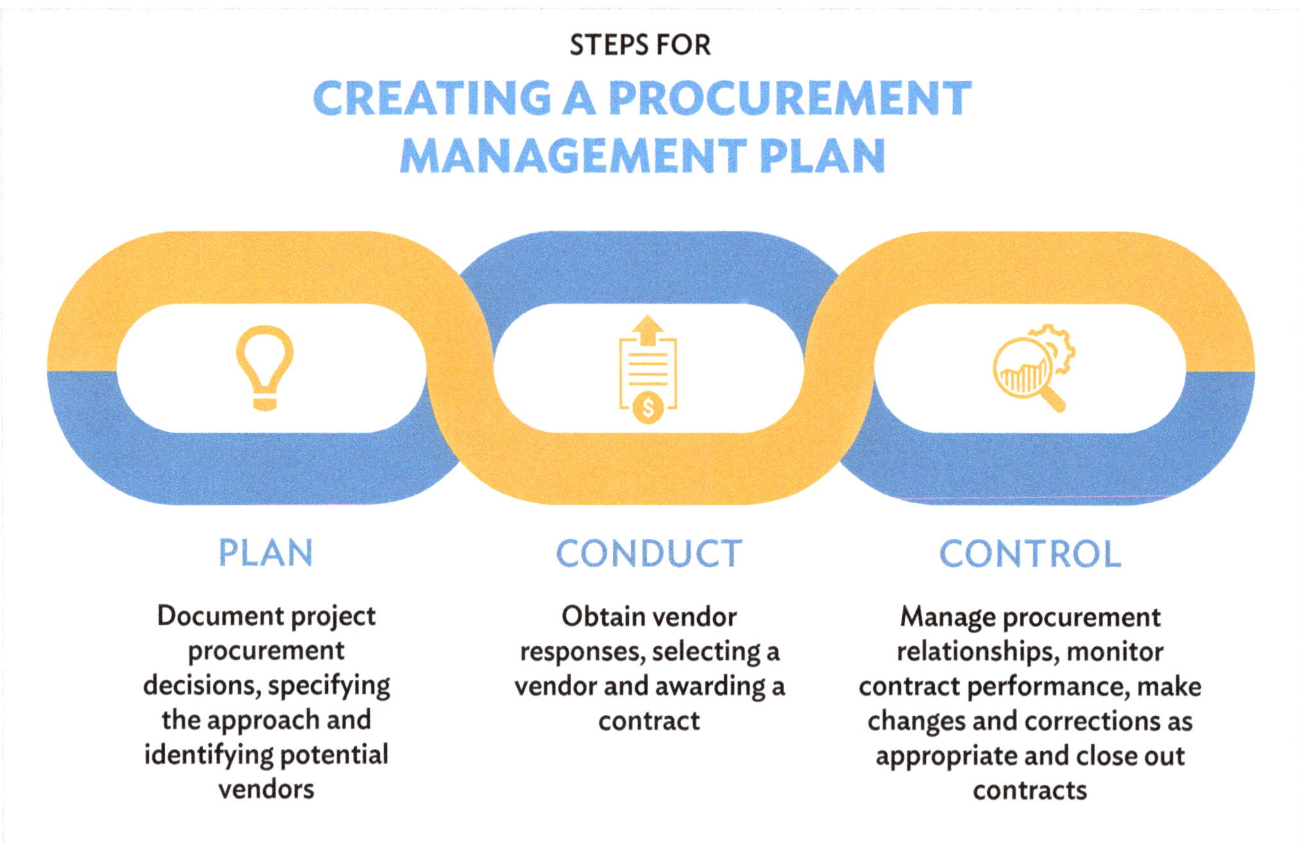

STEPS FOR
CREATING A PROCUREMENT MANAGEMENT PLAN
PLAN
Document project procurement decisions, specifying the approach and identifying potential vendors
CONDUCT
Obtain vendor responses, selecting a vendor and awarding a contract
CONTROL
Manage procurement relationships, monitor contract performance, make changes and corrections as appropriate and close out contracts

5.4.4 *Create a procurement management plan*

Most governments do not have the internal resources to build and maintain a digital HIS. Therefore, technology vendors will likely be contracted to develop and implement systems and provide ongoing support. Understanding how to evaluate vendor capabilities, write clear and defendable contracts, and manage contracts to completion are important financial management skills. A procurement management plan creates a framework for objectively selecting vendors with the right capabilities. If possible, a procurement professional should be a full-time member of the HIS team to assist with budgeting, vendor communication, scheduling and identifying contract risks. Procurement management includes the following steps (refer to footnote 25):

- **Plan:** document procurement decisions, specify the approach, determine evaluation criteria, and identify potential vendors.
- **Conduct:** call for proposals or quotes, obtain responses from vendors, evaluate responses, select a vendor, and award a contract.
- **Control:** manage vendors and contractors, monitor contract performance, modify and correct contracts as appropriate, and close out contracts.

5.5 Pitfalls

5.5.1 *Allow enough time for vendor selection*

Take time to identify appropriate vendors. Timelines should incorporate: identifying and documenting system requirements; developing a request for proposal (RFP); sending and receiving responses; reviewing and selecting short-listed candidates; performing due diligence on one or two preferred providers; undertaking contract negotiation and legal review. Depending on the size of the project, this process could take a minimum of 4 months (refer to footnote 23).

5.5.2 Do not under-estimate system maintenance costs

A common perception is that system maintenance is only about fixing defects. However, studies show that the majority of maintenance activities are for non-corrective updates—changes and enhancements to the system. Expect maintenance to range from 40% to 80% of the cost of the system build.[30] As systems are implemented, ensure there are sufficient funds to sustain and enhance existing software and hardware.

5.5.3 Do not expect an immediate return on investment

Studies show a return on investment in low-resource settings generally occurs after 3-5 years.[31] Sufficient initial and ongoing funding is, therefore, crucial to assure that the digital health system has enough resources to be sustainable until it starts to generate value for healthcare delivery. Otherwise, an argument could be made to use the budget for direct medical care.

5.6 Quick tip

Prioritize your system. Do the highest value work first.

Use an agile development approach to build and maintain the digital health system by building modules that are expected to return the highest organizational value first. Sometimes, this will require the work to be split up into smaller, demonstrable components.

5.7 Practice spotlight

Financial management in Tonga

The Ministry of Health in Tonga designed a two-phase procurement process for the selection of their digital health information system. First to seek expressions of interest that included gauging appropriateness of budget and to collect additional questions that could then be incorporated into the final terms of reference (TOR). The TOR was issued through an RFP and potential bidders responded with a full written bid that explicitly outlined whether their solution could provide the mandatory requirements and which of the secondary requirements would also be available. Following evaluation of initial bids, some bidders were invited to participate in a second stage, which involved presenting their solution in response to scenarios provided. The opportunity for the evaluators to see the system and be walked through the scenarios helped them understand what different users would see on screen and how easy the system was to navigate. This became a crucial step in the procurement process. The bidders were also required to respond in detail regarding training plans and change management. These areas were recognized as being as vital as the software system to success and bidders needed to show a strong cultural understanding and respond with solutions that would meet the needs of the country context. Knowledge transfer to IT professionals within the Ministry of Health was also a key element. The procurement design and execution were a lengthy process, however the time spent meant the final solution selected was one that met the current and future needs of the Ministry of Health and the people of Tonga.

Dr Siale Akauola—CEO, Ministry of Health, Tonga

30 Hanby, J. *Software Maintenance: Understanding and Estimating Costs.* Lookfar blog. Oct. http://blog.lookfar.com/blog/2016/10/21/software-maintenance-understanding-and-estimating-costs/.

31 Fritz, F., Tilahun, B, Dugas, M. 2015. Success criteria for electronic medical record implementations in low-resource settings: a systematic review. *Journal of the American Medical Informatics Association.* 22(2). March.

5.8 Resources and references

Ready. Set. Budget.

Resource: Digital Health Impact Framework
Using a digital health impact framework will help organize all inputs and outputs so that a strong cost-benefit analysis is produced, making decisions easier to justify

Reference: WHO toolkit on monitoring health systems strengthening—health systems financing
This toolkit outlines
- sources of information on health system financing
- core indicators
- using the financial indicators for health system strengthening.

Reference: Investing in digital health—costing tool
This tool provides the structure for a ground-up cost estimate of hardware and software for each facility based on type and size, health information exchange activities, interoperability costs, technical human resources costs.

Resource: IT software project budget template
More general than the costing tool, this template is a starting point for listing all potential project costs for an IT-type project. This template will need to be configured for your project.

Resource: Request for proposal evaluation worksheet
This template provides a framework for evaluating responses to a request for proposal or a request for quote from different vendors. The more specific you can be with your requests for proposals or quotes, the more detailed the responses from vendors will be. Define evaluation criteria and weightings for criteria such as experience, approach and price.

Resource: Request for Proposal (RFP) checklist
This checklist provides the critical topics that should be covered in your RFP.

6. WORKFORCE CAPACITY

6.1 Overview

Having a skilled, engaged and healthy workforce is a key requirement for effectively delivering healthcare services and realizing universal health coverage (UHC).[32] For digital health initiatives to be successful, clinical workers need to feel comfortable interacting with digital devices and seamlessly integrating digital elements into their workflow. Healthcare workers must be able to interpret, analyze and present data to make decisions based on evidence. ICT personnel must be able to design, develop, implement, and maintain the hardware and software that supports digital health solutions. Implementing and using digital health technologies requires a high level of aptitude—and the domain is constantly changing. Therefore, the workforce must have excellent analytical skills, be flexible and adaptable.

Digital health workforce development covers skills assessment, planning, management, policy making, and training of personnel on how to use and develop digital solutions. Governments and public and private organizations will need channels where they can find and provide ongoing training of skilled workers, both through the education system and by training existing workers.

6.2 Goals to accomplish

To find or develop a source of workers who have the technology and problem-solving skills to deploy and effectively use digital tools in a healthcare setting and to have enough funds to support capacity building efforts.

6.3 Importance

Why is it important to develop a trained digital health workforce?

Personnel with specific skills who can implement, manage, and use digital health systems are a critical prerequisite to successfully implement and sustain digital health systems within a healthcare organization.

6.4 Best practices

6.4.1 Plan, assess, and set policies; develop, track, and retain workers

Developing a workforce is a long-term endeavor that begins with setting a vision for the future. Assessing the current state of the workforce and the current health workforce education system allows you to understand the scope and type of skills needed by a country or an organization; it also allows you to assess diversity within your workforce, including gender diversity. As part of the process, standard occupational classifications (job descriptions) should be determined and detailed. These classifications outline minimum education and skills required to fulfil a job and should be set as policy for government workers. Once gaps are better understood, training programs through partnerships with universities, colleges, and healthcare institutions should be established to develop digital health programs to specifically fill workforce capability and gender gaps. This is especially important in the Pacific, where healthcare professionals are often trained in programs available in the larger countries in the region, such as Australia and New Zealand, ensuring that these regional training institutions provide digital health programs and modules that are relevant for all Pacific countries. As the workforce develops, it is important to track the number and skill level of workers disaggregated by gender, wages, staff turnover and truancy, as well as geographically tracking where skills are needed and where workers live. This tracking data will support decision-making on how to adjust the workforce mix to meet demand and how best to retain workers and provide them with a clear career path. There are a number of tools available to help through the workforce development process. See 6.8 Resources and references.

[32] Cometto, G., Buchan, J., Dussault, G. 2020. Developing the health workforce for universal health coverage. *Bulletin of the World Health Organization.* www.ncbi.nlm.nih.gov/pmc/articles/PMC6986219/.

6.4.2 Set workforce policy

Workforce development starts at the government level. Policies may include professional standards, licensing, and accreditations as well as salary grades and levels. Setting workforce policies requires an excellent understanding of the current labor market and a forecast of the type of jobs and number of people needed 5–10 years in the future (refer to footnote 32).

6.4.3 Ensure ongoing financial support

To support workforce development policies, adequate and ongoing funding must be allocated to building capacity for healthcare workers. Workforce development is a multi-year process; it is important to find reliable and continued sources of funding over a long-time horizon, even with changes in leadership. A costing exercise to identify current levels of expenditure, calculate the real cost of training, and project costs for different workforce development scenarios is important. This exercise will help policy makers understand where funds are spent and how they increase as the workforce is scaled up.[33]

6.4.4 Establish a human resources management system

Tracking the workforce in an electronic human resource system will provide data to identify gaps, plan, and evaluate changes in the workforce over time. Human resource systems can also collect data to support workforce performance management including staff appraisals, supervision, and productivity.[34] Human resources data can provide valuable evidence to policy makers that policies are having their intended impact and, if not, can provide input to help make adjustments.

6.5 Pitfalls

6.5.1 Do not assume technology skills transfer easily

An employee who supports hardware such as computers, servers, or networks does not necessarily have the same skills as someone who configures, runs and troubleshoots software.

While the skills for software and hardware are related, some skills, or indeed people, may not be able to transfer from hardware support to software support. If hardware staff are also required to provide software support, organizations must be prepared to invest in additional training and skills development. However, it is also important to note that even with additional training, some individuals may not be able to make the transition between skill sets.

6.5.2 Do not assume clinicians will be able and willing to perform IT tasks

If IT resources are scarce, it is not uncommon for healthcare organizations to expect clinicians to perform some IT tasks, such as rebooting hardware, fixing printers or monitoring software. While clinicians may be capable of performing these duties, the tasks may be considered outside their job scope and these expectations of stepping in to undertake IT tasks may erode morale.

6.5.3 Compensate ICT personnel competitively

Because individuals with ICT skills are in high demand and because supply is constrained, other sectors such as banking or telecommunications, with larger ICT budgets, are more easily able to hire skilled workers and compensate them at higher levels. To attract employees with strong technical skills, hospitals and other healthcare organizations must pay workers a competitive salary.[35]

6.6 Quick tip

Consider culture

When developing a national workforce development strategy, don't forget to think about culture. Developing a culture of learning, sharing, and equipping workers with tangible skills and critical thinking approaches will, in turn, raise the potential of the entire workforce.[36]

---

33 Tyrrell, A.K., Russo, G., Dussault, G. et al. 2010. Costing the scaling-up of human resources for health: lessons from Mozambique and Guinea Bissau. *Human Resources for Health.* 8, 14. https://doi.org/10.1186/1478-4491-8-14.

34 Capacity Project. n.d. *HRH Action Framework.* www.capacityproject.org/framework/hr-management-systems/.

35 Ogoe, H.A., Asamani, J.A., Hochheiser, H., Douglas, G.P. 2018. Assessing Ghana's eHealth workforce: implications for planning and training. *Human Resources for Health. November.* https://bit.ly/2LZbRN6.

36 Andriotis, N. 2017. The Workforce Development Strategy Tips to Make Your Staff Stand Out! *eFront.* https://bit.ly/2TCqOZS.

6.7 Practice spotlight

"The future of healthcare is digital", World Health Organization

The Director-General for WHO said, 'The future of healthcare is digital' and digital health is being embraced in the Pacific. Digital health investments are rapidly being deployed all over the Pacific where more than 25 countries are innovating and quickly finding out what works and what doesn't. Those responsible for data systems and digital health are eager to succeed and learn and apply good practices. There is a strong sense of know-how and resilience among the data and digital health community in the Pacific.

The Pacific Health Information Network (PHIN) has become a platform for health information and digital health professionals to exchange knowledge, leapfrogging into new frontier technologies, and building competencies and skills to scale and sustain investments. With partners like WHO, countries such as Fiji, Tonga, Samoa, Palau, Vanuatu, and Solomon Islands have developed strategies, architectures, and operational plans that have resulted in greater efficiencies and effectiveness of their health information systems. These digital investments in data platforms have strengthened the use of electronic medical records, mHealth applications, and disease surveillance. Innovations are making a significant difference. For example, support from UNICEF introduced drones in Vanuatu to deliver life-saving vaccines and medications across vast distances quickly and safely. Other partners such as ADB and Australia are making strategic investments supporting countries to finance, maximize, and scale-up the use of appropriate digital technologies.

Trainings, best practices, and ICT-certified techniques will continue to be needed and put into practice. Greater digital literacy among the health workforce is improving the uptake of digital interventions. However, the key to successfully operating, adapting, scaling, enhancing, and sustaining digital health investments is good governance and effective program management. Now is the time to enhance digital health competencies and build stronger institutional readiness to optimize investments for the greatest health outcomes through better service delivery models. PHIN and other peer-support and learning communities are eager to help with digital health achievements from across the Pacific.

Mark Landry

Regional Advisor, Health Information Systems

Regional Focal Point, Digital Health

Department of Health Systems Development

World Health Organization | Regional Office for South-East Asia | New Delhi, India

For digital health initiatives to be successful, clinical workers need to feel comfortable interacting with digital devices and seamlessly integrating digital elements into their workflow (photo by ADB).

6.8 Resources and references

The resources outlined in this section follow the workforce development process steps outlined and are tangible examples of output or tools to help with the process step.

Plan: Example of core digital health skills[37]

This capacity framework shows four key areas required for a skilled digital health workforce and the capabilities needed for each.

Table 3. Key capabilities for a skilled digital health workforce

No.	Domain	Summary of capabilities included in the domain
1.	Digital technologies, systems, and policies	Understand the purpose and function of digital health technologies and systems at local, state, or national levels, including a knowledge of legal, policy, and ethical implications
2.	Clinical practice and applications	Integrate digital health into clinical practice to deliver safe and quality care, including provision of best practice models of care
3.	Data analysis and knowledge creation	Use data and data analysis to inform, deliver, and improve health and healthcare practice at an individual, team, or systems level
4.	System and technology implementation	Participate in digital health implementation, evaluation, and codesign processes to drive improvement and stimulate change

Reference: **Assess workforce:** This workforce assessment tool covers a variety of skills including familiarity with devices and education and experience with ICT, digital health knowledge, and problem-solving abilities as well as understanding security, safety, and privacy. EU*US Self-assessment questionnaire

[37] Taken from: Brunner M., McGregor, D., Keep M., et al. 2018. An eHealth Capabilities Framework for Graduates and Health Professionals: Mixed-Methods Study. *Journal of Medical Internet Research, 20(5):e10229. May. doi:10.2196/10229.*

Set policy: Examples of digital health job descriptions

Three job types cover the key skill areas needed to develop and effectively use digital health tools for decision-making: Health Information Management, Health Informatics, and Health Information Technology.[38]

Table 4. Key positions needed to develop digital health tools for decision-making

Health Information Management (HIM) / Information Governance	Health Informatics (HI) and Data Analytics	Health Information Technology (HIT)

• Practice of acquiring, analyzing, and protecting digital and traditional medical information
• Trained in information management technology applications and workflow
• Management of health information and electronic health records
• Manage the quality of patient information
• Ensures the right information is available when and where it is needed
• Ensures information governance practices are in place and maintains the highest standards of data integrity, confidentiality, and security
	• Science that defines how health information is technically captured, transmitted and utilized
	• Analyzes health data
	• Advances decision support, usability and workflow practices
	• Practice and research focused with specialty domains:
	  • clinical practice
	  • management science
	  • management engineering principles
	  • healthcare delivery
	  • public health
	  • patient safety
	  • information science
	  • computer technology
		• Focus on Information and communication technologies
		• Develops, manages and supports the framework used to manage and exchange health information in a digital format
		• Works with software and hardware used to manage and store patient data
		• Support for electronic health records and other health technologies

Set policy: Example of digital health workforce policy

As part of Kenya's *Vision 2030* initiative to provide the highest attainable standard of healthcare for the country, a policy framework was developed. Workforce capacity development and training is one focus area of the framework.[39]

Policy Priority 1: Professional Training

To develop appropriate expertise in eHealth applications, the government will develop strategies for implementing the following interventions:

1. Provide continuous education, sensitization and technical support to users of eHealth system;
2. Provide for eHealth to be integrated in the existing education and training curricula at different levels of education and training.

Policy Priority 2: Capacity Building

To develop appropriate capacity for the adoption and utilization of eHealth products and services, the government will implement the following interventions:

1. Promote Continuing Professional Development through e-learning platforms
2. Organize training workshops and seminars from time to time with a view to impart new skills needed to use and maintain eHealth systems

[38] Taken from: American Health Information Management Association. 2014. *Equipping the Future eHealth Workforce through Global Curriculum Standards. Slide deck. U.S. Department of Commerce—International Trade Association Market Development Cooperator Program award #IT13MAS1120001.* www.ahima.org/~/media/AHIMA/Files/AHIMA-and-Our-Work/AHIMADOCMDCPOverviewcompressed.ashx.

[39] Ministry of Health. *Kenya National eHealth Policy 2016–2030. p. 24.* https://health.eac.int/publications/kenya-national-ehealth-policy-2016-2030.

Track: Example of freely available workforce management software

Track, manage and communicate your workforce using human resources software management tools such as iHRIS.

Train and retain: Examples of freely available training programs and short courses

- Health Informatics for Low- and Middle-Income Countries: Short Course for Health Information System Professionals, Measure Evaluation
- EU*US eHealth Work, Foundational Curriculum
- HITComp (Health Information Technology Competencies)— information on skills and competencies needed for different healthcare roles, levels and areas of knowledge
- Routine Health Information Systems (RHIS): A Curriculum on Basic Concepts and Practice – Syllabus and Facilitators' Guide, MEASURE Evaluation, January 2017

Reference: Global strategy on human resources for health: Workforce 2030, WHO, May 2016

Health informatics training in the Pacific islands region

Many universities in the region have Master and PhD programs as well as online courses and certification in health informatics and digital health. Search online to find the latest information available by these and other universities.

Table 5. Tertiary institutions in the Pacific region offering courses in health informatics and digital health

Type	University
Degree programs in health informatics/digital health	Bond University La Trobe University Macquarie University Papua New Guinea University of Technology RMIT Australia Swinburne The University of Auckland The University of Sydney University of South Australia Western Sydney University Master of Health Science
Graduate certificates	The University of Melbourne The University of Queensland
Online certifications and resources	Digital Health CRC-RMIT Future Learn Health Informatics New Zealand ITU Academy Digital Transformation Centers Initiative

7. CHANGE MANAGEMENT

7.1 Overview

Successful digital health transformation requires strong change management which may be defined as:

> *'...a strategic and systematic approach that supports people and their organizations in the successful transition and adoption of electronic health solutions. The outcomes of effective change management activities include solution adoption by users and the realization of benefits'.* [40]

Technology itself is rarely the greatest challenge to implementing a digital health system. Right from the start, digital health implementations must be user-centric and implemented in partnership with healthcare providers. Integrating technology into healthcare services changes how healthcare providers and operation managers do their work, may cause disruptions, and can negatively impact care (refer to footnote 39). New workflows may not be intuitive and some people may feel they will be replaced by technology. Change management supports healthcare providers and patients to integrate technology into their daily tasks and helps them understand the benefits of the change.

7.2 Goals to accomplish

Digital transformation of healthcare processes requires process reengineering to optimize and simplify these processes using technology. Change management must be integrated into project planning to ensure staff understand and agree with the benefits of technologies and are trained in how use and integrate them into their daily work.

7.3 Importance

Why change management is important

Change management is all about assuring adoption. Creating and following a change management plan will increase the speed of adoption, utilization and proficiency of users. In turn, this will avoid unnecessary costs, improve access to information and lead to the realization of system benefits more quickly (refer to footnote 39).

7.4 Best practices

7.4.1 Identify and use a change management framework

The elements of a change management framework include: governance and leadership, communications, stakeholder engagement, training and education, workflow analysis and integration, and monitoring and evaluation.[41] Activities within these elements are focused on people, to successfully adopt a digital health system and realize its benefits.

Figure 3. Change management framework

Source: https://health.eac.int/publications/kenya-national-ehealth-policy-2016-2030

[40] Canada Health Infoway. 2013. A Framework and Toolkit for Managing eHealth Change: People and Processes. March. https://bit.ly/2ZobwKn.

[41] Jarocki, T. 2013. PMI Project Management versus Change Management: Similarities, Overlaps and Differences, *Journal of Change Management Community of Practice*, ProjectManagement.com. Webinar. June www.projectmanagement.com/videos/286316/Project-Management-vs-Change-Management.

7.4.2 Integrate a change management plan into your organization's project plan

A strong project plan must include a change management plan that addresses organizational and process changes as a result of a digital health implementation. Anticipating where people may be impacted and putting in place communication plans, appropriate incentives, and initial and ongoing training programs will go a long way toward assuring that users will make an effort to adopt the system.

7.4.3 Ensure processes are owned by the healthcare providers in partnership with IT

Establish a strong partnership between the IT implementors and the healthcare providers throughout the project. By including all stakeholders in decision-making and seeking input from end users will help to create buy-in.

7.4.4 Build a case for change

The value and benefit of implementing a digital health system is not always obvious. Government leaders and clinical executives must communicate a vision for how the system will positively benefit the end users and the value it will create for the organization. Making a case for change weights the positive and negative consequences of implementing digital health systems. Articulating the case for change can be done through workshops, focus groups, interviews, field studies, and data and opinion gathering activities.

7.5 Pitfalls

7.5.1 Invest in change management

It is important to identify a change manager and supporting team as part of your digital health implementation project. The team should include individuals from parts of the organization that will be impacted by the digital health system implementation. Their responsibilities include developing key messages, identifying target audiences, drafting a communication plan, emails, and newsletters. They should be given time from their regular job functions to work on change management activities.

7.5.2 Include change management in your risk management plan

When putting a project risk management plan together, do not forget to include risks that focus behavior such as resistance to adopting software, political influence, cultural barriers, poor communication, insufficient sponsorship, wrong rewards or recognition or disengaged governance.

7.5.3 Provide sufficient training and technical support after the implementation

Training and technical support is usually provided at the time of the initial implementation. Funding must be allocated to ongoing support in the form of training for new staff members, fixing software defects and supporting hardware.

7.6 Quick tip

Engage the most vocal clinical opponent of the transformational strategy in the process. Listen to their ideas and ask them to help improve the strategy and implementation.[42]

[42] Nieves, R. 2018. '*3 tips on managing change in a hospital's digital transformation*'. Elsevier Connect, February. https://www.elsevier.com/connect/3-tips-on-managing-change-in-a-hospitals-digital-transformation.

7.7 Practice spotlight

Change management in Tonga

The rollout of a new technology solution is more than software and hardware—the users of the system and the ability for them to adapt to a new solution are critical. In Tonga, the importance of change management as part of the implementation of their digital health information system has always been a key requirement for success. Change management readiness workshops were held across Tonga with health workers to focus on people change rather than technology and identify the changes they were most looking forward to, the concerns they had and any resistance or fear of change that existed. This early work, done before the terms of reference was finalized, provided the Ministry of Health with important information about what the health workforce needed to make the digital health information system implementation a success. Training on the system use was identified as just one element. An understanding of privacy of information, how data would be used and how that could help health workers and patients is important. For each role, various levels of change were identified and this led to a requirement to provide basic computer literacy training through to more advanced data analysis training depending on roles. The recognition of cultural context was vital and the establishment of change champions was a crucial step to liaise between users and implementors and ongoing learning and use of the system. The importance of change management cannot be underestimated. Tonga recognized this and started their change management journey well before a system was even decided. The change champions provide a way to ensure change management continues well after the system goes live.

Dr Siale Akauola—CEO, Ministry of Health, Tonga

7.8 Resources and references

Resource: Change Management Plan template

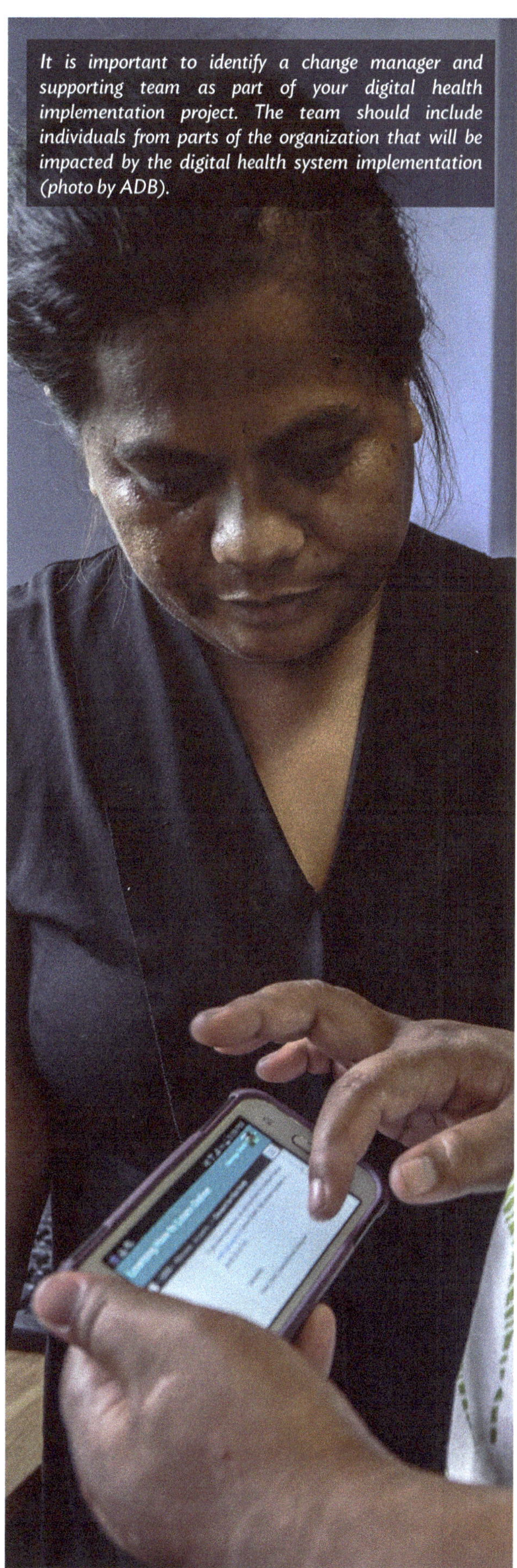

It is important to identify a change manager and supporting team as part of your digital health implementation project. The team should include individuals from parts of the organization that will be impacted by the digital health system implementation (photo by ADB).

8. ACHIEVING SCALE

8.1 Overview

The following definition helps to give context to what it means to successfully scale-up digital health systems across different technologies and different stakeholder groups:

> *"Digital health is considered to be successfully scaled-up when it is embedded or institutionalized into the workflow of a health system's service delivery or into a recipient's daily habits."*[43]

Scaling up requires all of the components for a successful digital health system implementation to be brought together: leadership in ministries and work groups, strong policies, human and financial resources, and digital technologies that are robust and enhance quality care. The ability to scale digital health systems is tightly linked to the sustainability of the system. To ensure sustainability of a technology, it is important to understand the social, environmental and economic implications on a health system before implementing it.[44]

8.2 Goals to accomplish

Most organizations find scaling-up digital health projects challenging. It requires an enabling environment that must happen at the national level and includes adopting national standards, policies, regulations and laws, ICT in health services, and policies for developing a capable workforce. All of these factors should be addressed and tied to a national digital health strategy, which should include sustainable healthcare models for the future. Achieving scale takes time—mostly years—and therefore funding and planning should be aligned accordingly.

8.3 Importance

Why achieving scale is important

Pacific island countries are committed to developing digital systems to helping in achieving universal health coverage.[45] To achieve this goal, successful pilot implementations must be scaled and new projects must interoperate with existing technology.

8.4 Best practices

8.4.1 Select a practical and sustainable framework to guide your institution

The ability to scale-up digital health systems is complex and organizational and economic aspects are just as important to manage and monitor as the technology aspects. The framework suggested by PATH is straightforward and can be referred to as part of a digital health strategy and scale-up planning (refer to footnote 43).

8.4.2 Develop a sustainable economic model

Develop short-term and long-term funding plans as part of your digital health strategy, right from the start. Well-planned, large-scale digital health initiatives can take anywhere from 5-9 years before positive returns are realized.[49] Therefore, governments need to commit early to investing in digital health and working with donors and private companies to find sustainable funding for successfully scaling up. Strong digital health policies will help focus where and how funds should be applied to optimize value. An economic appraisal will help leaders and planners understand the socioeconomic and financial impact of their digital health strategies (refer to footnote 27).

43 Wilson, K., Gertz, B., Arenth, B. and Salisbury N. 2014. *The journey to scale: Moving together past digital health pilots.* Seattle: PATH.

44 Fanta, G.B., Pretorius, I., and Erasmus, L. 2015. An evaluation of ehealth systems implementation frameworks for sustainability in resource constrained environments: a literature review. *International Association for Management of Technology, 2015 Conference Proceedings*

45 CISCO. 2019. *Reaching 650 Million: How Digital Technology is Key to Achieving Universal Health Coverage in ASEAN.* www.cisco.com/c/dam/global/en_sg/assets/pdfs/healthcare.pdf.

Figure 4. Path framework for scaling eHealth systems

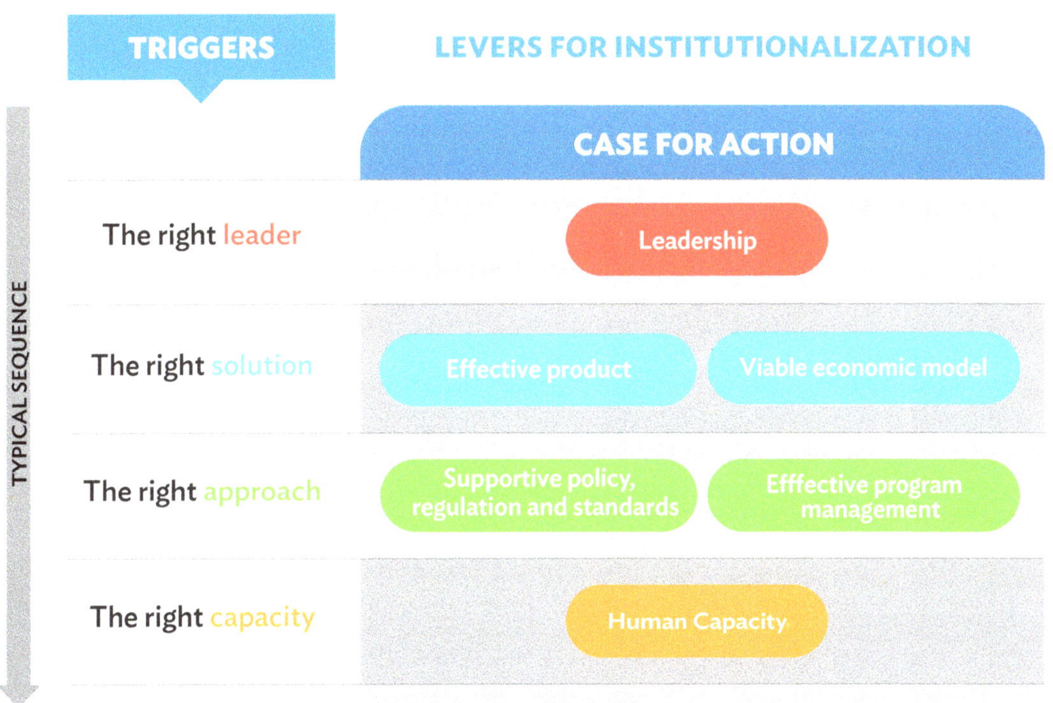

Adapted from Wilson, K., Gertz, B., Arenth, B. and Salisbury N. 2014. The journey to scale: Moving together past digital health pilots. Seattle: PATH.

8.4.3 Focus on interoperability

While pilot digital health projects have generally been successful, when taken to scale, they can be costly and inefficient due to a proliferation of discrete or independent systems (refer to footnote 27). It is important to establish interoperability guidelines and policies as early as possible to limit the number of incompatible components and costly rework—interoperable systems save time and money. For successful scale-up, government agencies must establish and support interoperability requirements as part of a digital health strategy.[46] Using standards such as HL7 and FHIR, which are specifically tailored for healthcare systems, should be adopted. Assistance on how to set policy may be found at the Asia eHealth Information Network (AeHIN.org) and help to design and test your interoperable solution may be found at the Standards and Interoperability Lab Asia.

8.4.4 Understand the digital foundations for Universal Health Coverage

To achieve scale and provide quality health coverage for all citizens, as well as track public health statistics for planning, evaluation, and emergency response, a unique national ID is a foundational requirement.[47] Closely related is safeguarding protected health information (PHI) that can be used to identify individuals. Patient health information is at the center of every system transaction and it must be kept secure and used appropriately. Understand how policies and implementation of these foundational aspects impact scaling-up.

46 WHO. 2012. 'The bigger picture for e-health', *Bulletin of the World Health Organization*, Volume 90, Number 5, May, pp. 321–40.

47 Stahl, M., Roth, S. Thorell, L., and Parry, J. 2016. On the road to universal health coverage: Every person matters, *ADB Briefs*. https://www.adb.org/sites/default/files/publication/183512/uhc-every-person-matters.pdf.

8.4.5 Find strong leaders or champions

A strong leader or champion, who can articulate the vision and benefits of a digital health system and recruit leaders from other disciplines who share the vision and values, is paramount to a successful scaling up. As a group, these individuals will determine the appropriate technology; make long-term funding commitments and engage donors; foster partnerships and engage all stakeholders; implement the technology; and be early adopters willing to test innovations and set the stage for success, while being well informed and making data-driven decisions (refer to footnote 43).

8.4.6 Scale up the healthcare workforce at a country level

Scaling up digital health systems must include scaling up human resources: identifying new skills required, training existing employees, and hiring additional staff where needed. For long-term sustainability of human resources, domestic resources should be mobilized, only using external resources to temporarily fill gaps. Financing may be needed to cover the initial and ongoing costs of additional staff.[48]

8.5 Pitfalls

8.5.1 Ensure you have evidence of impact on healthcare delivery

Many digital health components and technologies seem to make intuitive sense, so individuals and leaders may not feel evidence of positive and lasting impact on healthcare delivery is required. However, it is essential that organizations scaling up their digital health technologies demonstrate, through pilot implementations or examples from other countries, that healthcare services are enhanced and also cost-effective. Before new technologies are scaled, they should be evaluated by a broad set of stakeholders for value to healthcare delivery and operations (refer to footnote 46).

8.5.2 Country-level ownership and leadership

Ownership at the country level is critical for health systems, and local capacity is essential. Most organizations do not have the required institutional or individual expertise to effectively scale up and maintain digital health systems. To address this issue, establish a separate unit within the Ministry of Health specifically focused on health information, ensuring it is staffed with people with the appropriate skills.[49]

8.6 Quick tip

Calculate the total cost of your digital health system, not just the cost of the technology

Estimate the total cost of ownership of the digital health system, not just the cost of technology. Total cost of ownership estimates the total scaled-up cost of developing and implementing the technology or product, as well as any costs per user, such as the purchase of mobile devices, the cost of training and reduced productivity of health providers while systems change.[50] Use tools such as the one provided by the Standards and Interoperability Lab-Asia to help identify and calculate costs.

[48] WHO. 2008. *Financing and economic aspects of health workforce scale-up and improvement: framework paper: Alliance financing task force.* October. www.who.int/workforcealliance/knowledge/publications/taskforces/frameworkpaper.pdf.

[49] Huang, F., Blaschke, S., Lucas, H., 2017. Beyond pilotitis: taking digital health interventions to the national level in China and Uganda, *Globalization and Health.* https://globalizationandhealth.biomedcentral.com/articles/10.1186/s12992-017-0275-z.

[50] WHO. 2015. *MAPS Toolkit mHealth Assessment and Planning for Scale.* https://apps.who.int/iris/bitstream/handle/10665/185238/9789241509510_eng.pdf?sequence=1.

What is a national health ID?

A national health ID (NHID) is a unique identifier for patients across multiple providers and organizations. An NHID is essential for the successful implementation of Universal Health Coverage linking all health, wellness, and disease-prevention activities within a country. It is particularly important when providing health services during a pandemic like COVID-19 where patient tracking and access to patient records is critical. An NHID should be a meaningless but unique number and should not contain any patient-identifying information such as name, initials, location, or date of birth.[51] The NHID becomes the master key that unlocks other sources of the patient's identification and health history.

Why have a national health ID?

1. To positively and accurately identify an individual or patient
    - For patient care information into a paper or electronic record
    - For the delivery of care such as diagnosis, treatment, medication
    - For administrative functions such as billing and payment
2. To identify information
    - For collecting, aggregating and analyzing information for population-based research and planning
3. To support the protection of privacy and confidentiality through accurately identifying and de-identification
4. To reduce healthcare operational costs by supporting more efficient records management and information sharing.[52]

What is the role of digital health governance required when establishing a national health ID?

Establishing an NHID policy framework and implementing a system that supports it at a national level is a complex process that requires strategic planning and coordination.

The following list outlines some of the questions that should be asked when deciding to implement a NHID:

- Will a new identifier will be created independently or will another existing national IDs be used?
- What will be the format of the national health ID?
- How will the national ID be distributed? Will it be centrally managed?
- How will a national patient registry be established and function?
- How will paper-based patient number generation be linked to an electronic generated patient ID?
- How will a user be assured that the ID is correctly owned by an individual? Will biometrics we used to identify a patient?
- How will the number and any associated personal information be kept secure, confidential and private?
- How will different systems be linked to the national patient registry?
- Which ministries will provide the infrastructure and overall oversight?
- What's the implementation and communication strategy?
- How will the technology be supported?
- How much will the development, implementation and ongoing support cost?

Because there are so many facets to establishing an NHID—multiple stakeholders, patient safety, new technology, and a significant investment in human and financial resources—a digital health governance structure is necessary. National oversight and standards are needed for information governance, country policies, data collection, data storage, data transfer, and data access. The Unique Health Identifier Tool Kit[53] provides a structured process to assess the existing legal, institutional and political framework, the available technology infrastructure and the existing and health sector registries and identifiers. Using the information gained through the assessment the country can make an informed plan for the implementation of an NHID.[54]

---

51 Ritz, D. 2016. Caring for #EVERYCHILD. Video 2 of 3. https://vimeo.com/156650602.

52 Beck, E.J. et. al. 2018. Developing and implementing national health identifiers in resource limited countries: why, what, who, when and how? *Global Health Action*, Vol 11.

53 ADB. 2018. *Unique Health Identifier Assessment Tool Kit*. May. https://www.adb.org/documents/unique-health-identifier-assessment-toolkit.

54 UNAIDS. 2014. *Considerations and guidance for countries adopting national health identifiers*. Joint United Nations Programme on HIV/AIDS.

8.7 Practice spotlight

Papua New Guinea's eNHIS

With increasing population growth and 87% of the population living in remote and rural settings,[55] Papua New Guinea (PNG) faces hurdles delivering healthcare. In 2011, PNG published a National Health Plan and in 2017 the NDOH delivered a supporting plan for digital health.[56] Their goal is to provide world-class, digital-enabled healthcare services across the country over the next decade. The strategy outlines three key goals for the PNG digital health system and how these goals will be achieved in a challenging environment:

1. Improved quality, safety and experience of care
2. Improved health and equity for all populations
3. Best value for public and private health system resources.

As part of their plan and as discussed in Institutional readiness, PNG's Rural Primary Health Services Delivery Project, overseen by the NDOH, aims to strengthen the national electronic health system (eNHIS). After an initial roll-out to five provinces, an assessment showed that the eNHIS established a significant and positive change in data collection, quality, timeliness, and data use. Since the assessment, the NDOH has steadily been rolling out an enhanced eNHIS and building capacity to achieve scale. eNHIS has been rolled-out to an additional seven provinces, prioritized based on COVID-19 outbreaks and in provinces where there is significant cross-province migration. A major barrier to continued scale-up and roll-out is funding.

Despite funding setbacks, eNHIS is beginning to achieve scale, evidenced by high reporting rates in 7 out of 12 provinces where it has been implemented. The system is showing much higher reporting rates, and reaching 95% on-time reporting. This is largely driven by strengthened capacity of the provincial health information officers who follow up to ensure complete and timely data entry from the facility level to the national system.

Figure 5. Triple-aim framework for quality improvement

Achieving scale of PNG's eNHIS is largely driven by identifying a champion at the provincial level to drive sustainable change. A management training program has been implemented to strengthen capacity across provinces. Similarly, a need to up-skill provincial data officers' roles to include improved analytical skills has been identified in order for data collection officers to become data users and data use advocates.

PNG will likely see continued scaling up through continued development of the workforce, activities-based budgeting targeting eNHIS roll-out and user acceptance, and development of supporting standards and policies.

Robert Akers, Project Manager

PNG Health Services Sector Development Project & Rural Primary Health Service Deliver Project

[55] World Population Review. n.d. Papua New Guinea Population. https://worldpopulationreview.com/countries/papua-new-guinea-population

[56] Government of Papua New Guinea. 2017. *The National eHealth Strategy 2017–2027.*

8.8 Resources and references

How sustainable is your framework?

Many digital health systems are unable to be sustained beyond their pilot phase. Sustainability challenges for digital health implementation include weak ICT infrastructure, lack of funding, a shortage of technical skills to support technologies brought from developed countries, and the introduction of technologies that were not specifically developed for implementing the context of developing countries.[57]

Resource: The Conceptual framework for sustainability and scale of digital health poses questions and makes suggestions for actions to address these issues across the three components of a sustainable digital health system: environmental, social and economic.

Figure 6. Conceptual framework for sustainability and scale of eHealth systems

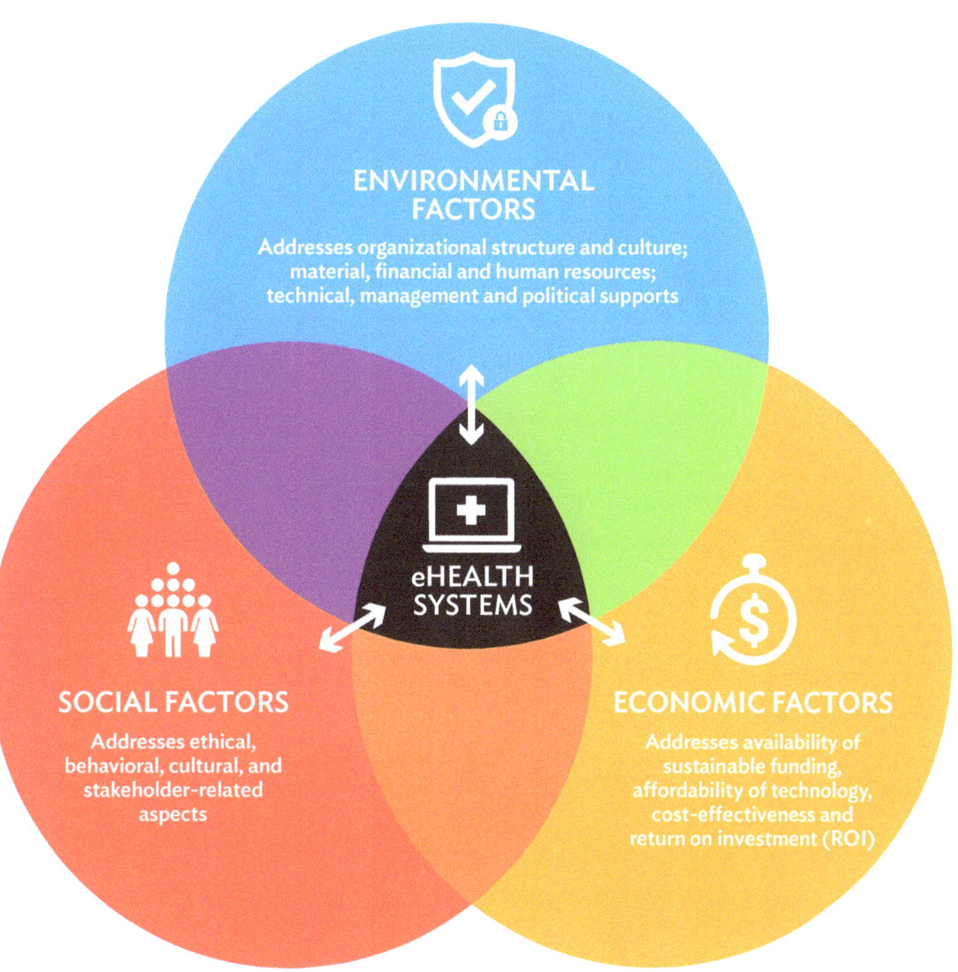
CONCEPTUAL FRAMEWORK FOR
SUSTAINABILITY AND SCALE OF eHEALTH SYSTEMS
ENVIRONMENTAL FACTORS
Addresses organizational structure and culture; material, financial and human resources; technical, management and political supports
eHEALTH SYSTEMS
SOCIAL FACTORS
Addresses ethical, behavioral, cultural, and stakeholder-related aspects
ECONOMIC FACTORS
Addresses availability of sustainable funding, affordability of technology, cost-effectiveness and return on investment (ROI)

57 Fanta, G.B. 2015. An Evaluation of eHelath Systems Implementtaion Frameworks for Sustainability in Resource Constrained Environments: A Literature Review. In *International Association for Management of Technology IAMOT 2015 Conference Proceedings.*

Digital health systems are complex, involve a wide set of stakeholders, impact existing healthcare delivery processes and often require an entirely new skill set for technology and healthcare staff (photo by ADB).

TECHNICAL

TECHNICAL
CONTENTS

9. SYSTEM ARCHITECTURE

9.1 Overview

"Systems are a class of software that provide services to applications and other systems. The term is associated with core operational technologies that automate work, control equipment and provide data processing services."[58]

Systems perform actions like saving patient data. Systems may be integrated with other software or other systems, for example, verifying a unique patient number from a central registry. Systems may access data through an Application Program Interface (API). Software systems run on physical equipment or system infrastructure.

Information system architecture is a formal definition of the various components of a system including the business rules that define how components of the system work, the technologies used, and the organizational structure of the components within the system. The architecture encompasses both the software and hardware that make up the system.

Figure 7. Information architecture encompasses software and hardware

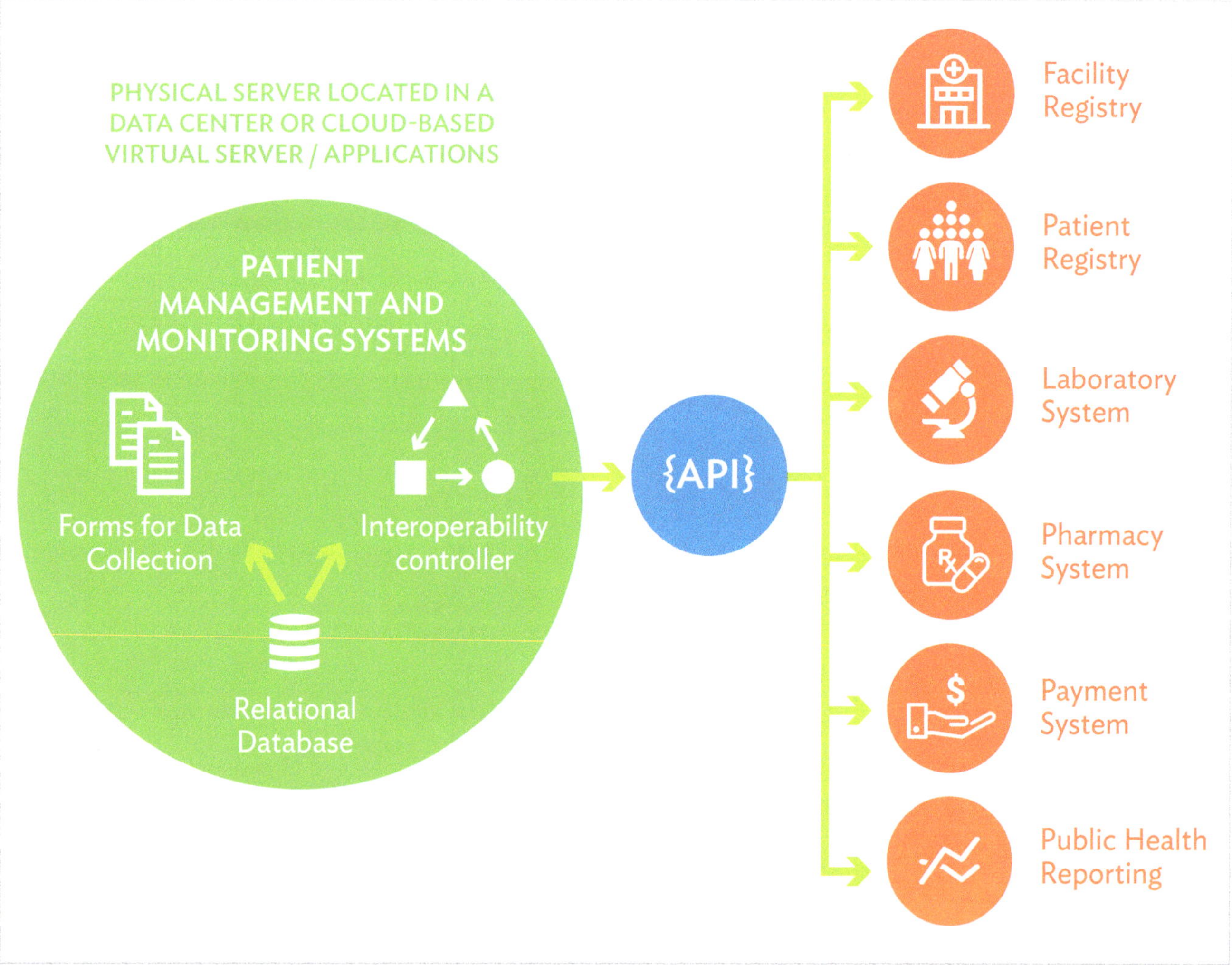

PHYSICAL SERVER LOCATED IN A DATA CENTER OR CLOUD-BASED VIRTUAL SERVER / APPLICATIONS

PATIENT MANAGEMENT AND MONITORING SYSTEMS

Forms for Data Collection

Interoperability controller

Relational Database

{API}

Facility Registry

Patient Registry

Laboratory System

Pharmacy System

Payment System

Public Health Reporting

[58] Simplicable. n.d. *4 Examples of System Architecture. Simlicable.com.* https://simplicable.com/new/systems.

9.2 Goals to accomplish

A high-priority goal is to design a digital health system that can run a universal health coverage program. This system should include designing interoperable and connecting components with central data repositories. This means that different healthcare processing services within the system can securely access and update patient records. With the internet connectivity challenges in the Pacific islands region, systems should be able to accommodate "occasionally connected" systems where data is stored locally and connected to a central repository periodically when the internet is available. In areas with no internet connectivity, a system could include secure storage of patient history on smartcards to allow patients to carry their latest health records with them when they visit different healthcare services.

9.3 Importance

Why a properly planned system architecture is important

Early decisions about system architecture design are the most difficult to get right because assumptions about software and hardware performance and user interaction and use are yet to be validated. These early decisions will have the highest impact on the system design and, usually, are the hardest to change later. Factors such as expected growth needs, software licensing models, data security and privacy, technical human resource capacity, stakeholder requirements, and overall cost of ownership should be considered and documented as part of the system architecture phase of implementing a digital health system.

9.4 Best practice

Figure 8. Principles for digital development

Principles for Digital Development

 **Design With the User**

 **Understand the Existing Ecosystem**

 **Design for Scale**

 **Build for Sustainability**

 **Use Open Standards, Open Data, Open Source, and Open Innovation**

 **Be Data Driven**

 **Reuse and Improve**

 **Address Privacy and Security**

 **Be Collaborative**

Source: https://digitalprinciples.org/principles/

Incorporate the Principles for Digital Development in all your digital health projects.

The Principles for Digital Development consist of nine living guidelines to help technology innovators and software developers to build and implement user-centric, high quality and useful technology solutions. Endorsed by over 200 organizations, the principles were developed by a global digital health community and informed by lessons learned by technology practitioners. They are meant to be updated over time and refined to maintain relevance as technologies and innovations change and develop.

By applying these principles to digital health projects, services will be enabled more quickly, be built for sustainability, and ultimately reach more people. Regardless of the project size, sector or technology, these best practices can help organizations reach their development goals.

9.4.1 Design the system architecture for future growth

Typically, with any information system, the volume of data grows over time, enhancements are made to existing services and new services and facilities are launched. Information systems evolve rapidly and some of what is implemented today may become obsolete or inadequate in 3–5 years' time or even less.[59] Therefore, it is important to design with the future in mind. To make the most of the investment, implementation should take into account the overall planned architecture and possible expansion. Ideally, lay out the entire "to be" future system and then prioritize short-term and long-term essential components for the system to be successful.

9.4.2 Design or purchase extensible and configurable software

Configurable software systems allow the system administrator or user to turn on or off features or modules for everyone or just for certain users; allows features to be customized for the users' needs, such as select lists that display in patient health record forms. While some systems may require significant effort to configure the software, these kinds of systems are extensible and can be changed as needs change in a workflow process without new code development. Configurable software allows the implementation to be done in phases.

9.4.3 Choosing between open source and proprietary software applications

The decision to use open source or proprietary software applications depends on what your organization is trying to accomplish, the availability of human resources, and the technical skills of your team members. The decision may also be impacted by the policies of your country or organization. Some proprietary software vendors may offer an open source version their programs, such as Microsoft's Net Framework for Software Development, Dimagi's CommCare Mobile Form Builder, or Oracle's MySQL Database. While open source technologies do not require licensing, reducing your requirement to "lock-in" to a particular provider, the need for highly skilled technology expertise, and the quality and security of the open source technology may require verification to ensure it meets healthcare standards.[60]

Table 6. Pros and cons of open source and proprietary software applications

Open source pros and cons

Pros	Cons
Lower cost—no licensing fees	Requires skilled software developer to make updates or run the software
Standards-based software protocols	Minimal or no technical support with generally poor technical documentation
Completely customizable code base	Code-base complexity and often challenging to learn
Questions answered from a global community of users and developers	Few large, financially strong open source software vendors

Proprietary pros and cons

Pros	Cons
Professional user interface—easier to use	Cost of the initial and/or ongoing licensing
Product stability targeted to large-scale enterprises	Customization generally requires costly professional services
Routine updates with bug patches and new features	Closed data sources with limited APIs for data exchange
Technical support services from the software provider	Switching software vendors can be difficult and costly

[59] Gersh, L. 2013. 'The Velocity of Obsolescence'. *Forbes.com. July.* www.forbes.com/sites/lewisgersh/2013/07/29/the-velocity-of-obsolescence/#3256f72a6596.

[60] Munoz-Cornejo, G., Seaman, C.B., and Koru, G. 2009. An Empirical Investigation into the Adoption of Open Source Software in Hospitals. *International Journal of Healthcare Information Systems and Informatics. January.* www.researchgate.net/publication/220168739_An_Empirical_Investigation_into_the_Adoption_of_Open_Source_Software_in_Hospitals.

9.4.4 Use technology appropriately

While the internet has improved our ability to communicate data, some areas are yet to experience the benefits that come with high speed 24x7 connectivity and power availability.

In low resource environments, it is prudent to design data collection systems on paper first and only digitize what is useful for decision-making, striking a balancing between effort and return. Even in an e-first system, it is important to have paper systems to fall back to in case of electronic system failure so that service disruption due to, for example, power outage or computer failure is kept to a minimum.

Not every problem can be solved with technical approaches and, sometimes, it is appropriate to use a non-traditional method to solve a challenging issue. For example, for a facility that is in an occasionally connected environment with poor or expensive internet access, it may be appropriate to store patient data onsite and only connect to a central database to transmit aggregate data intermittently or incrementally. If the site has no internet access at all, data can be periodically backed up to external storage and couriered to a connected office to integrate with a central repository. It may also be appropriate to collect less data electronically and to use SMS decision support systems (DSS) or interactive voice response (IVR) systems for reporting to a central system.

To store and transmit sensitive data, it is essential to apply sound security principles to protect patient information. The ultimate goal is to design a platform for secure health information data collection, storage, and information use that is appropriate for the environment, minimizes data collection effort, and maximizes information use. System design must consider a security architecture to allow for data to be shared by individuals with appropriate access.[61]

9.4.5 Factor in redundancy

Where it is not possible to rely on national infrastructure such as a power grid, integrating alternative energy systems such as solar, wind, and battery backups can solve outage problems. In addition, particularly where e-first systems are deployed to remote areas, it is important to have a contingency plan, such as reverting to paper data recording, in the event of technical failure so that client services can continue. Resources also need to be budgeted to catch up on data entry when systems are online again.

9.4.6 Design with the user in mind

Systems should be designed with all users in mind. Users include central decision makers, facility staff and patients. Mapping individual user journeys when engaging with the digital system helps identify user needs and preferences. User-centric design considerations include access to the internet, preferred device for viewing and entering data, and preferred user-interface for the software itself. For example, even the most robust centralized systems can fail if it is difficult for remote facilities to use it because of slow internet. By ensuring that data is easy to collect and aggregate and that generate reports, user adoption will be greater, leading to cleaner and more useful information for decision-making.

9.4.7 Document the system architecture

Documenting the system architecture with diagrams and text descriptions helps with knowledge sharing and promotes transparency. There are many approaches and open source tools, such as Draw.io, for architecture diagrams and database entity relationship, available for documenting architecture, but no one approach fits all. Documentation should include descriptive narratives as well as diagrams that effectively convey the principles the organization is trying to implement. Documentation must be updated as the architecture evolves.

[61] Sulaiman, R., Sharma, D., Ma, W., and Tran, D. 2008. *A Security Architecture for e-Health Services. International Conference on Advanced Communication Technology. March 2008.* https://www.researchgate.net/publication/4325306_A_Security_Architecture_for_e-Health_Services.

9.5 Pitfalls

9.5.1 *Don't design with too much detail*

System architecture should convey general, high-level design, without too much technical detail, unless explaining fundamentals. It can be tempting to impose a specific approach or technology, but using more generic details allows more flexible options in solutions design. For example, the architecture may describe the philosophy and general technical details of system integration, allowing some users to implement their existing systems with their preferred method rather than mandating specific technical approaches.

9.5.2 *Don't design with too little detail*

Sometimes it may be necessary, particularly with fundamental principles such as privacy and security, to be more specific. For example, it is prudent to describe a minimum required level of encryption for storing sensitive data and transmitting data across the public internet.

9.5.3 *Ensure environmentally appropriate designs*

With health information systems, what is appropriate for a large, wealthy corporate firm is unlikely to be appropriate for a small environment with limited resources and geographically distributed systems. Design should account for environmental limits such as power infrastructure, available skills and human resources, equipment availability, and support. For example, it is unwise to implement an online application for remote facilities that have expensive, slow, or unstable internet access.

9.5.4 *Involve all stakeholders*

When designing a health information system architecture, it is important to consult with stakeholders and experts from all levels of the health system and ensure diversity of stakeholders. Stakeholders include male and female program managers, clinicians, and community health workers, both centrally based and at the facility level. Patients with different health needs, such as mothers, caregivers, and youth should also be included. Inputs from all stakeholders assures that key technology needs are documented and integrated to create an architectural design that is appropriate and can grow with demand. This kind of information would be gathered during the digital health assessment phase.

9.6 Quick tip

Don't overcomplicate things; simple is often the best

Certain approaches that are simple, but have the right resources, can be highly effective in enhancing the overall efficiency of digital health systems. One example is establishing a central health facility data exchange where details of national health facilities such as name, location, contact details, management organization, facility head, and services provided are collated in a central database that is accessible by any system requiring this information.

Many health information systems use some form of facility registry for referrals and cross-facility reporting. Centralizing health facility data exchange reduces duplication of effort by ensuring a single, up-to-date registry of all national facilities. However, it is important to establish clear roles for collating the database. Part of creating those roles may include a curated 'crowd-sourced approach' that allows suggested edits by experts close to the field, while being approved and integrated centrally having regard for diversity of contribution.

9.7 Spotlight

Architectural assessment and review—Standards and Interoperability Lab-Asia, Lab Director

Architectural assessment will depend on the maturity of the digital health components. For countries in the early stages of digital health development, I suggest first establishing a digital governance body. Once digital health governance is in place, then architectural structures can effectively be discussed. Given the state of IT infrastructure in the Pacific island region right now, and the fact that countries are geographically separated, a federated architecture should be considered.

This type of framework has worked successfully in the Philippines for the implementation of Universal Health Coverage. In federated systems, each island has its own health information exchange that works independently from the other islands. Integration of these federated hubs can be done at the most progressive island (or capital). For the Philippines implementation of Universal Health Care, the country is divided into health service delivery networks, with each network working independently. The Department of Health of the Philippines integrates the data to ensure that patient data is available across the entire system. So, if a patient needs to access services within their primary network or outside at a different health facility, their data is available to healthcare providers when needed.

I highly recommend that all systems, both legacy systems and new ones, undergo an architectural review. The architecture should be part of the digital health strategy and governance structures, which is why governance is so very important. Governance bodies should mandate compliance to an agreed upon technology architecture and to the standards that the architecture espouses.

Philip Christian Zuniga
Standards and Interoperability Lab-Asia, Lab Director

9.8 Resources and references

Reference: Principles for Digital Development

Designing your "house": elements of system architecture

Reference: Software Architecture in Practice. Second Edition: Len Bass, Paul Clements, Rick Kazman, Addison Wesley, 2003.

This book introduces the concepts and best practices of software architecture providing practical guidance from engineering and business perspectives. Using case studies from real systems, the authors demonstrate how organizational requirements drive software system performance, availability, security, and compatibility with other systems. They empathize that designing the right architecture has a high return on investment in terms of software quality, schedule, and cost. If the design is incorrect, it is difficult to fix.

The authors provide techniques for designing, building, and evaluating software architectures with a strong emphasis on understanding quality requirements. Advice on how to re-use architectural assets and how to document software architecture is also included. Throughout the book, discussions about software architecture is related to the business cycle and needs.

Reference: Open Health Information Exchange (OpenHIE) is a Community of Practice that specifies interoperable data standards in the international healthcare context. OpenHIE is a framework of open source components for national-level health data exchange. OpenHIE:

- enables large-scale health information interoperability
- offers freely available standards-based approaches and reference technologies
- support countries' needs through peer technical assistance communities.

To get involved sign up at: https://ohie.org/#involved.

Reference: Interoperability Reference Architecture This document is the first edition (2010) of the Interoperability Reference Architecture for New Zealand. It describes a high-level future state architecture to support the interoperability requirements of the National Health IT Plan.

Reference: Documentation in Software Architecture This article discusses the benefits of documenting a system architecture, the types of diagrams, and tips that are useful for producing well-articulated software architecture documentation.

Reference: Free Online Desktop Diagramming Tool The tool is easy to use has templates needed to create a system diagram and files are easy to share.

10. INTEROPERABILITY AND INTEGRATION

10.1 Overview

When two or more information systems or components can exchange and make use of information based on standards, then the systems are considered "interoperable".[62] There are four levels of interoperability that contribute to an increased and seamless integration and interoperability of systems: foundational, structural, semantic and organizational.[63]

Digital health information systems are complex ecosystems made up of these interoperability levels that serve the needs of different users with different sources of data. Every healthcare system has its own requirements and, typically, a variety of software components is required to perform all of the functions needed in a healthcare system. Therefore, it is imperative that a digital health system can interoperate with other systems that are designed to perform a specific function, such as supply chain management, human resource management, or laboratory management.

Designing and implementing interoperable systems is not easy. It requires human resources with specialized technical skills to establish systems that can exchange data and also requires ongoing funding to maintain systems. The promise of Universal Health Coverage, which requires health information exchange across multiple national systems, means that governments and supporting organizations must make careful investments to support standards development and interoperability.[64]

Figure 9. Four levels of interoperability that contribute to integration and interoperability of systems

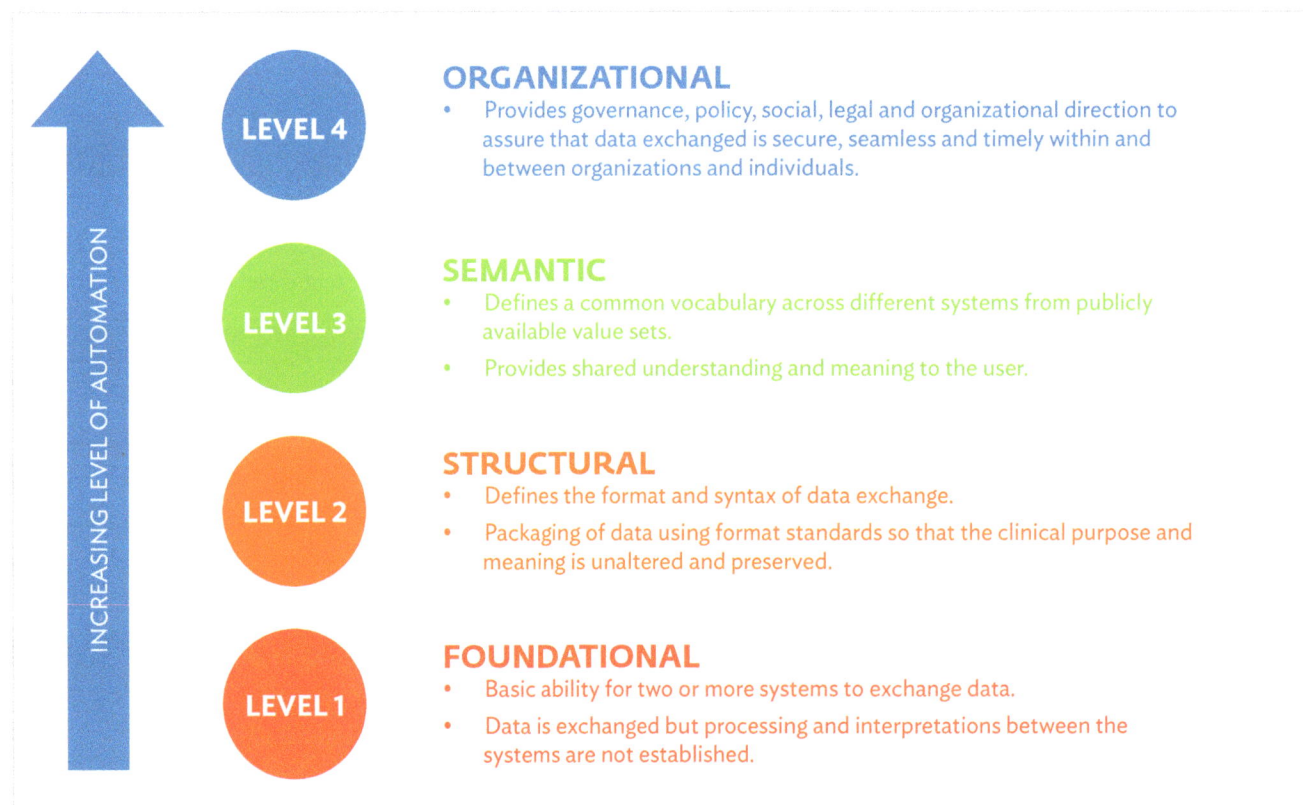

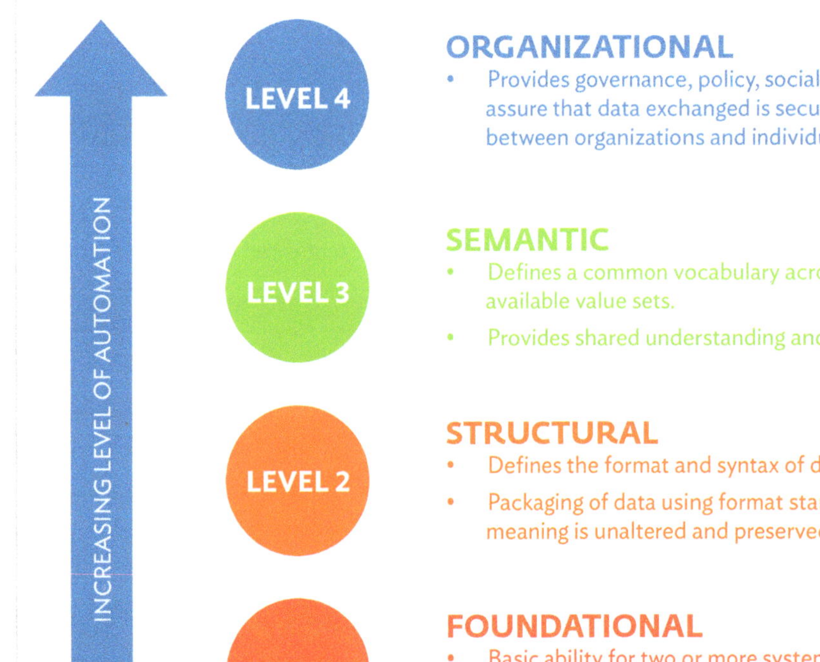

ORGANIZATIONAL

- Provides governance, policy, social, legal and organizational direction to assure that data exchanged is secure, seamless and timely within and between organizations and individuals.

SEMANTIC

- Defines a common vocabulary across different systems from publicly available value sets.
- Provides shared understanding and meaning to the user.

STRUCTURAL

- Defines the format and syntax of data exchange.
- Packaging of data using format standards so that the clinical purpose and meaning is unaltered and preserved.

FOUNDATIONAL

- Basic ability for two or more systems to exchange data.
- Data is exchanged but processing and interpretations between the systems are not established.

62 MEASURE Evaluation. 2019. *Health Information Systems Interoperability Maturity Toolkit: Users' Guide Version 1.0. January.* www.measureevaluation.org/resources/publications/tl-17-03a.

63 HIMSS. n.d. *Interoperability in Healthcare.* www.himss.org/resources/interoperability-healthcare.

64 Drury, P., Roth, S., Jones, T., Stahl, M., and Medeiros, D. 2018. *Guidance for investing in digital health. ADB. May. No. 52.* www.adb.org/sites/default/files/publication/424311/sdwp-052-guidance-investing-digital-health.pdf.

10.2 Goals to accomplish

A foundational goal is to design and deploy digital health systems based on sound interoperability, integration principles, and messaging standards. Standards-based systems are more sustainable; sub-systems and individual applications can be scaled, upgraded, and replaced independently without having to replace entire systems.

10.3 Importance

Why interoperability and system integration are important

Ultimately, interoperability is about the availability of up-to-date, accurate, and reliable data to support work tasks and decision-making by end users. Being able to reference authoritative data sources, such as for clinical, pharmaceutical, and other commodities; human resources; infrastructure; and geographic data allows multiple departments and systems to use data without maintaining duplicate siloed systems. It also ensures that the authority for data sources is responsible for maintaining that data set, which greatly enhances data quality while reducing overall effort.

10.4 Best practice

10.4.1 Planning and top-down design

Thoughtful planning and a top-down approach are required to successfully implement a central repository for key reusable data such as a health facility registry, a central patient registry, and a health information exchange. Clearly defined roles, responsibilities, and budgets for maintaining central systems is essential to their success. In addition, establishing a robust communication plan for reporting updates and issues are essential for the system to remain current and useful. An electronic ticketing system is also useful for all parties using the data to track and report issues and changes.

10.4.2 Data communication standards

Shared data communication standards are essential for interoperability and integration. Systems are considered interoperable when one system successfully sends or pulls data from another and uses it in the correct context. With this data exchange, the security, foundational, structural, and semantic requirements have been met.

Figure 10. Data communication standards

DATA COMMUNICATION STANDARDS

When exchanging data, the sending and receiving systems must be able to communicate.

Messages generated must be verified as coming from a trusted system and the data request in a readable format.

The second system must send the data back conforming to the standard and the versions on the requesting system.

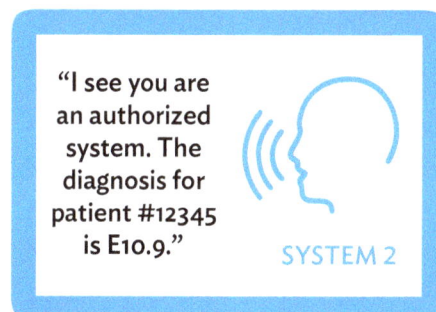

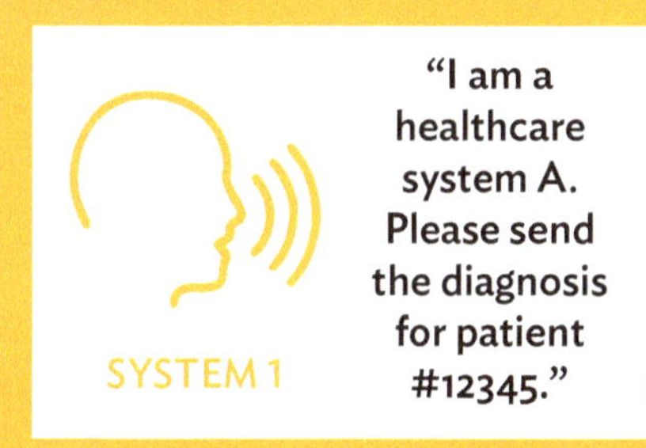

"I am a healthcare system A. Please send the diagnosis for patient #12345."
SYSTEM 1
"I see you are an authorized system. The diagnosis for patient #12345 is E10.9."
SYSTEM 2

The use of well-established standards for both systems makes the process of data exchange much easier and faster to implement.

Standards address Level 2 — the structure or format of the data exchange message and Level 3 — the semantic or meaning of the contents of the data being exchanged.

A popular Level 2 standard for data communication between applications is Representational State Transfer or REST. The REST architecture is typically used for transmitting data, usually over the internet in various formats including the popular Javascript Object Notation (JSON) data format. Another popular protocol is the Simple Object Access Protocol (SOAP) and the associated extensible markup language (XML) data format. Both REST and SOAP are agnostic to the type of data being transferred.

For health-specific data, HL7 has been in use for many years as a framework for data interoperability. Previous versions have either been so permissive (V2) as to prevent interoperability or been so complex and difficult to implement (V3) that too few systems took it up. Fast Healthcare Interoperability Resources (HL7 FHIR), (currently version 4), is an attempt to address the previous problems and is receiving rapid uptake across the world's health software community. HL7 FHIR can simplify integration and interpretation of data, but still requires architectural rigor and close attention in the application of the standard to implement it correctly and achieve technical and clinical benefit.

HL7 as part of the OSI 7-layer stack, is often coupled with broad ontologies such as SNOMED-CT and classifications such as the well-known International Classification of Diseases, Tenth Revision (ICD-10) and the Logical Observation Identifiers Names and Codes (LOINC) common to all laboratory systems. The combination of the capture of clinical data using an Ontology or Classification with a FHIR "wrapper" is currently driving a major surge in the transfer of clinical data with active payloads and is set to see a more agile and modular future for clinical data and the systems seeking to use it.

Another example of interoperability is the need to integrate clinical imaging, such as X-ray or CAT scan images along with their description, into electronic health records. Using standards like HL7 FHIR, picture archiving and communication systems (PACS) can be integrated into clinical workflows such as ordering a radiology test, capturing the image, documenting the results and archiving the image with secure data exchange.[65]

10.4.4 Document the technical specifications

Clear documentation of the technical specifications of interoperability components is important, including context, data formats, encoding, and behavior to allow external parties to be able to easily understand and use them. Documentation should be "living" and preferably should form part of a national knowledge base for integration across the healthcare sector. A well-documented data dictionary for each digital health application is essential for understanding the definition of the data elements and ensuring equivalence across systems.

10.5 Pitfalls

10.5.1 Ensure adequate resources and good communication

Systems integration requires collaboration and communication across departments and partners implementing data systems. If a centralized approach is not maintained or the authority responsible for coordination is not well resourced, it becomes difficult to implement systems effectively.

10.5.2 Adequately plan and do not overcommit

Planning for interoperability within a national health information system needs to be purpose-driven with realistic goals that are appropriate for the context, particularly resources. For example, in settings with few resources and poor connectivity, it may not be appropriate to establish a central patient registry or health information exchange. A resource-intensive system or trying to focus on complex and unproven areas of information in a low-resource environment will inevitably fail.

10.5.3 Do not make data security an afterthought

It's best practice to 'design in' security protocols and establish legal agreements between exchanging entities to assure patient data security and privacy when implementing data exchange.[66] It is imperative to know what data will be shared, who will have access to this data and for what purposes. Legal permissions must be put into place based on job function.[67] Examples of security and data use concerns include being

65 Orlova, A., Bourquard, K., and Parisot, C. 2017. Understanding User Needs for Interoperability: Standards for Business Cases in eHealth, *Journal of AHIMA 88. No.7 (July): 34–37.*

66 Berryman, R., Yost, N., Dunn, N., and Edwards, C. 2013. Data Interoperability and Information Security in Healthcare. *Transactions of the International Conference on Health Information Technology Advancement, 26 October.* https://scholarworks.wmich.edu/ichita_transactions/26.

67 Siwicki, B. 2020. Privacy & security perspectives: Interoperability, prospects for HIPAA refresh, more. *Healthcare IT News. June.*

able to uniformly identify patients, losing patient data or transforming it during exchange, misinterpreting data due to semantic differences, as well the security of information during data transmission and at rest. Regular audits should be performed to monitor data security and privacy.

10.6 Quick tip

Plan for interoperability from the start

Often, different systems may be developed or implemented in parallel by different parties. While it is tempting to want to connect everything, it may not be possible with limited budgets and time. By implementing systems that allow data to be imported or exported via file transfer or by implementing service-based application programming interfaces (APIs) from the start, you can ensure that other systems can easily integrate at a later stage when resources are available.

10.7 Spotlight

Standards and Interoperability Lab-Asia

I want to highlight the great work that is being done at the Standards and Interoperability Lab-Asia (http://sil-asia.org/). The SIL-Asia is a reference interoperability lab established by ADB. We were established to provide interoperability guidance and support in the region. Our services cover: tooling—we work on tools to achieve interoperability; teaming—we work with developer teams to understand and help frame their project goals; training—we provide technical capacity development support to expand their technical skill and leadership; and testing—we test applications to ensure standards compliance. Currently, all our services are paid by Technical Assistance from ADB. However, in the future, we hope that governments will support the work at this interoperability lab. Some countries have already established their own labs.

Philip Christian Zuniga

Standards and Interoperability Lab-Asia, Lab Director

10.8 Resources and references

Reference: Health Level 7 Fast Healthcare Interoperability Resources (HL7 FHIR) FHIR is a standards framework that uses building blocks called "resources" and metadata to create a flexible, modular format. This format exchanges data using web-based API technology such as HTTP and RESTful protocols. Software developers with strong open source language and API skills will find FHIR easy to understand, but training will be required to effectively implement FHIR. This site provides some guidance to help get new implementers started on their path to successful implementation. Many countries are moving to HL7 FHIR to take advantage of its ability to exchange integrated unstructured and structured information. https://fhir.org/

Reference: 5 Things to know about HL7 FHIR This article outlines the Top 5 things to know about this upcoming standard that some hope will help solve many current issues in interoperability.

Reference: What's the difference between SOAP and REST? This article outlines the difference between REST and SOAP, two different approaches to online data transmission.

Reference: Health Information Systems Interoperability Maturity Toolkit, Measure Evaluation The toolkit provides a maturity model, an assessment tool, and a users' guide.

Reference: Standards and Interoperability Lab-Asia SIL-Asia is a health interoperability lab that provides technical and capacity-building support to countries. The lab is established by the Asia eHealth Information Network, with support from ADB.

11. SECURITY, PRIVACY, AND CONFIDENTIALITY

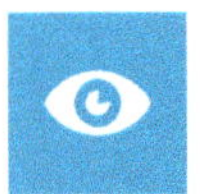

11.1 Overview

Protected health information (PHI) is any information in a medical record that can be used to identify an individual. PHI usually includes identifying information such as name, address, birth date, sex, and national ID number so that the patient can be accurately identified. Examples of PHI include a medical record, laboratory report, or hospital bill.[68]

Patient health information is at the center of every system transaction. Security, privacy, and confidentiality of this information are interrelated and cover all aspects related to running digital health systems.[69] In addition to establishing governance and policies around the access to and handling of PHI, the systems themselves must be secure. Cybercrime is on the rise with increased instances of fraud, theft, identity theft, and even acts of terror. "Cyber hygiene", which is the practices and processes that ensure systems, computers, and devices are maintained and configured as securely as possible to protect the patient data and organization assets.

11.2 Goals to accomplish

The primary goal should be to establish cyber hygiene best practices to protect sensitive health-related information, ensure privacy for patients and healthcare workers, and protect the reputations of organizations working for improved health outcomes. Practical steps can make systems more robust and staff can be educated on how to understand the evolving risks of connected systems. Each best security practice should be supported by policy and process for ongoing monitoring and maintenance.

11.3 Importance

Why security and privacy of patient health information is important

Protecting digital health information, system security, patient privacy, and confidentiality is of the utmost importance to stop criminals stealing data for financial gain, for example from submitting bogus health insurance claims to shutting down entire healthcare systems while demanding a ransom, to third parties giving employers information about health conditions without the consent of the patient. Individuals should be able to use healthcare services and be confident that their personal information will remain private and their identity protected. This is particularly important in smaller communities where most people know each other and interact with each other almost daily.

68 US Department of Health and Human Services, (n.d.) *Health Information privacy, Guidance Regarding Methods for De-identification of Protected Health Information in Accordance with the Health Insurance Portability and Accountability Act (HIPAA) Privacy Rule.* www.hhs.gov/hipaa/for-professionals/privacy/special-topics/de-identification/index.html#protected.

69 Spigel, L., Wambugu, S., and Villella, C. 2018. mHealth Data Security, Privacy, and Confidentiality: Guidelines for Program Implementers and Policymakers, *MEASURE Evaluation*, January.

11.4 Best practice

Figure 11. National policies for security, privacy, and confidentiality

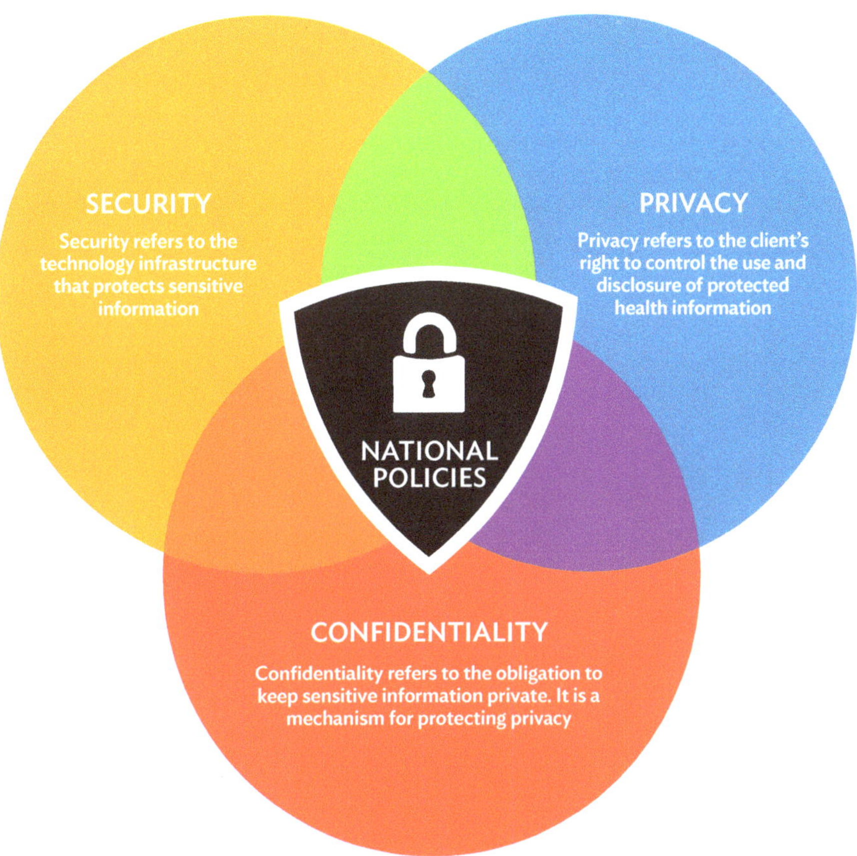
NATIONAL POLICIES FOR
SECURITY, PRIVACY, AND CONFIDENTIALITY
National policies central functions with security, privacy, and confidentiality of protected health information
SECURITY
Security refers to the technology infrastructure that protects sensitive information
PRIVACY
Privacy refers to the client's right to control the use and disclosure of protected health information
NATIONAL POLICIES
CONFIDENTIALITY
Confidentiality refers to the obligation to keep sensitive information private. It is a mechanism for protecting privacy

Adapted from Spigel, L., Wambugu, S., and Villella, C. 2018. *mHealth Data Security, Privacy, and Confidentiality: Guidelines for Program Implementers and Policymakers*, MEASURE Evaluation, January.

Privacy and security policies

At a national, regional and organizational level, it is important to put privacy and security policies and processes in place, including identifying staff to oversee and monitor that policies are being followed. The list of policy areas spans from the physical location of the organization to the software and communications with third parties. Dedicated resources such as a privacy officer should oversee all ongoing activities related to the development, implementation, and maintenance of patient privacy policies.

Together with selected staff members, the team should identify areas of concern within the organization and actively look for ways to improve and enhance privacies and security approaches. Start small and build up.

Table 7. List of potential privacy and security policies to be developed

Policy area	What the policies should cover
Employee responsibilities	Employee requirements such as wearing personal identification on premises, prohibited activities, handling of email, reporting software malfunctions and security incidents, handling of sensitive and confidential information, and other employee-centric policies.
Identification and authentication	User login IDs and passwords. Issuing confidentiality agreements, setting appropriate access control on software, review of employee access rights and termination processes.
Network connectivity	Telecommunication equipment and services including land and mobile phone, T1/network lines, third-party connections and contracts, and firewalls.
Malicious code	Use of antivirus software, new software distribution process, and software ownership.
Encryption	Use and type of encryption; encrypted email, files via attachment or file transfer protocol (FTPS); and secure sockets layer (SSL) for web traffic.
Building security	Building access for employees and owners.
Telecommuting	Occasional and full-time employees who work remotely from home, including required equipment and hardware configuration.
Wireless usage/transportable media	Use of wireless access points in hotels, airports and homes and software requirements; transfer of data via USB and other devices.
Retention/destruction of medical information	How to retain and when to destroy records.
Disposal of external media/ hardware	How to properly dispose of media and old equipment.
Change management	Tracking and documenting changes in networks, systems, workstations, including software releases and vulnerabilities.
Audit controls	Tracking and recording computer activities.
Information system activity review	Processes for conducting periodic operational reviews of system activity, including user accounts, file access, audit logs, etc.
Data integrity	Verification that patient information has not been altered or destroyed in an unauthorized manner.
Contingency/disaster plan	Formal practices to address unexpected damage or downtime of one or more systems.
Security awareness and training	Type and frequency of security policy and procedures training for new and existing employees.
Security management process	Ongoing assessments of potential risks and vulnerabilities of the systems and processes.
Emergency access	Formal and documented process for employees to enable unauthorized workforce members to get access in a patient emergency.
Sanction policy	Who and under what circumstances workforce members are denied access or have access revoked.
Employee background checks	Conduct formal reference and background check of employees and/or contractors.
Breach notification procedures	The process of notification of affected individuals in the case of a breach, including the patient, employees and any other individuals affected.

Source: www.healthit.gov/resource/information-security-policy-template

11.4.1 Take a risk-based approach

Adopting a risk-based approach means looking at your digital health system holistically across all aspects of your industry and your specific environment and determining the frequency and severity of security risks. Systems should then be configured or modified to meet a minimum standard across all areas of your organization. Steps to take for a risk-based approach include the following:

1. Undertake an audit of your internal and external risks.
2. Identify weaknesses in your cybersecurity ecosystem and address them in order of priority.
3. Identify roles and responsibilities for all staff in maintaining cybersecurity and ensure these staff are equipped with adequate tools and training.

11.4.2 Implement the "three As" of secure systems

Systems that store sensitive data must properly implement the "three As" of secure systems: authentication, authorization, and accounting.

Authentication is the process of recognizing a user's identity—it is the step in the system access process (usually login) that determines that the person operating the system is who they say they are. For example, entering a password when logging on is an authentication process. The three major categories of authentication are as follows:

1. Something I know, for example a password.
2. Something I have, for example a mobile phone.
3. Something I am, for example biometric identification such as a fingerprint or retina scan.

Where possible, sensitive data should be secured with at least two authentication factors (2FA), at a minimum. Some 2FA methods use SMS to send a temporary code to the user's phone. More secure systems use mobile-based applications or automated calling systems to supply authentication codes. 2FA systems may also use security keyfobs that display a time-based, one-time password.

Authorization is the process of verifying and controlling the features and functions an authenticated individual has access to. For example, an accountant may have access to financial records, but not to medical records, while a clinician may have access to medical records, but not financial records. Principles of least privilege, which means only assigning access to users who require specific systems or features within a software product, to undertake their role. Furthermore, this least privilege approach should be applied to access to workstations, server rooms or other locations where sensitive records are stored. Be careful not to apply "administrator access" to this equipment where it may be easy to access the entire system. By applying least privilege approach, the opportunity for users to accidentally or intentionally view sensitive data or execute malware is reduced.

Accounting is the process of logging activity on a system, such as remote access to a server by the IT team or updates to medical records in an electronic medical record (EMR). Accounting adds a layer of accountability and traceability to systems for retrospective analysis if they are compromised or suspicious activity is detected. For sensitive data, the user ID, date/time, and component of the system that has been accessed should be automatically logged. Logging can also incorporate alerts (e.g., mobile alerts) to managers when sensitive systems are accessed.

11.4.3 Develop a comprehensive Disaster Response and Recovery Plan

As electronic systems are increasingly used for communication, record keeping, analysis, and decision-making, it is important to understand the risks and be prepared for downtime in the event of ICT "disasters" such as data loss, corruption, hardware and software failure, security breaches, and malware. Strategies should be environment- and resource-appropriate and may incorporate some of the following:

- redundant (failover) servers
- off-site backup
- spare hardware (workstations, servers, networking equipment, etc.)
- alternate internet connectivity
- paper-based record backup
- technical support agreements.

Business impact analysis should take into account the impact of various threats and disaster scenarios and define appropriate recovery time objectives and recovery point objectives (RTO/RPO) to continue working with minimal interruption in the event of disaster.

In addition to the recovery process, a disaster response plan should define appropriate communication plans for various scenarios. The communication plans should specify parties affected by any downtime or data breaches and information conveyed about the disaster should be audience-appropriate.

Testing a disaster recovery plan will help to ensure that each step works as intended and that the system can be recovered in the event of a real disaster. Plans should also be revised over time to remain appropriate as systems evolve.

11.4.4 Set up system monitoring and update processes

When new hardware and software systems are implemented, security requirements are usually addressed and meet current standards. Security vulnerabilities and cybercrime are always evolving and monitoring processes must be set up and assigned to a security officer to check systems on a scheduled basis. Examples of system checks might be verifying that the default admin user account password has been changed, patching or upgrading software to protect them for the latest malware, reviewing audit logs and investigating anomalies, and ensuring that all data is backed up, encrypted and moved to an off-site location.

Managing data systems in an offline or occasionally connected environment can be challenging. In remote locations, it may not be practical for IT staff to service the site regularly. Therefore, a carefully planned service schedule should be implemented with advanced notice to ensure site staff are prepared. A "lights-out" management (LOM) system can be considered to allow for remote administration and monitoring,[70] and software updates can be downloaded on removable media to install during these visits to keep systems up-to-date. Secure off-site backup may be difficult for remote locations. If removable media is used for daily or weekly backups, ensure it is encrypted to mitigate the risk of data leaks through loss or theft.

11.4.5 Use principles of least privilege access to digital and physical environments

Using principles of least privilege means only assigning access to users who require specific systems to undertake their role. Assigning access to more people than necessary puts your data at risk by increasing the potential "attack surface". The risk relates to both the employees themselves, and increasing the potential for your network and systems to be unknowingly exposed to malware from workstations and mobile devices. For example, when malware is released in a privileged account, access is granted to whoever is assigned to that account. It is common for system administrators to simply apply "administrator" access to workstations to make them easier to maintain; however, this approach is high risk is terms of cybersecurity. System administrators need adequate training to ensure they understand the risks and adhere to the principles of least privilege.

Another way to reduce your attack surface is to not collect or store sensitive data unnecessarily. Not all data is useful, and it is not always useful to collect sensitive data. Less data reduces your risk.

Principles of least privilege can be applied to physical environments as well. For example, you should apply the principles of least privilege to an office where only authorized employees have access to a server or a room where sensitive records are stored.

11.4.6 Encrypt your data

Encryption is the process of encoding data so it is not human-readable and that only authorized people who know how to "unlock" the encryption can access the encrypted data. Typically, data encryption falls into two categories: encryption of data at rest and encryption of data in transit. Data at rest is data stored on a physical medium such as a hard drive, database, flash memory, or other media. Encrypting data at rest ensures that if physical hardware or data files fall into the wrong hands, they will be unreadable without proper authorization. All sensitive data should be encrypted at rest as a standard policy. This can be undertaken by the operating system or by the application that uses the data, or both. A common, easy-to-remedy threat is data stored on USB drives. USB drives are common and often used to copy data from one system to another. Not only do they introduce the risk of transferring malware between systems, but their size and portability mean they are prone to being lost, stolen, or used for personal reasons. If it is necessary to use USB drives to store or transfer sensitive data, ensure the drive is encrypted with a password to mitigate the risk of data loss.

Data in transit is data that crosses a network such as a local area network (e.g., office network) or a wide area network (e.g., the public internet)—usually between a client

[70] Rouse, M. 2007. *Lights-out management (LOM). SearchDataCenter.* https://searchdatacenter.techtarget.com/definition/lights-out-management.

computer and a website or web application. Encrypting data in transit ensures that data cannot be intercepted over networks or public internet by unauthorized individuals. Encrypting data in transit usually involves installing cryptographic certificates issued by a trusted authority. All sensitive data systems hosted on web servers should use a Public Key Infrastructure certificate system and Transport Layer Security to ensure that data is only readable by authorized systems.

Cloud- or office-based servers used over the internet should never be used for system administration without adequate security. Services such as SSH (Linux Secure Shell) or RDP (Windows Remote Desktop) are popular targets for cybercrime and should not be exposed via the internet. A certificate-based virtual private network (VPN), such as the free OpenVPN, can be used as an additional layer of defense. Only the VPN interface is exposed, and a private certificate is required for access to the VPN in addition to a user name and password.

11.4.7 Have systems for backing up and restoring data

Ensure that all data is backed up off-site and offline regularly. When determining how often to back up, ask yourself, "What would be the effort and cost of collecting or reconstructing lost data?" In smaller clinics, data may be able to be recreated from paper records, but in a larger facility with point-of-care systems, it may not. Larger facilities may require daily backups that are encrypted and stored off-site in a cloud-based server. Smaller clinics may choose to back up weekly; however, if a natural disaster results in data loss, paper records may also be unrecoverable. Ensure it is possible to rebuild systems and reload data backups in the event of disaster or theft.

In environments with offline or occasionally connected remote systems, data can be backed up to encrypted, removable media, such as a removable hard drive or USB flash drive, and sent to a central site for integration or analysis—a process known as "sneakernet". This ensures that data is periodically backed up and stored off-site and made available for reporting at a central level.

11.4.8 Segment networks

Networks (wired or wireless) should be segmented into logical departments to separate data and minimize your attack surface. For example, computers used for accounting can be logically separated from computers used in the clinical department that run patient data systems. By segmenting networks, if a computer in one segment is compromised, information from other segments cannot be accessed.

11.4.9 Train staff in cyber hygiene

Cyber-hygiene training is important, especially for new staff. Refresher training and certification should be undertaken for existing staff at least annually. Training can be computer-based or online, so staff do not need to be off-site to update their skills and knowledge. A number of online cybersecurity training courses are available, including free and subscription-based courses.

Some of the fastest growing cyber threats involve social engineering, where employees are tricked into performing actions based on a convincing communication, such as an email, SMS, or even a phone call. Clear policies and processes should be documented on how to handle requests for money or sensitive data, with a verification step validating the requestor and the transfer of funds or information. It is not uncommon for email accounts to be spoofed or compromised and used by criminals to request, for example, wire payment requests. A phishing test is used by security and IT professionals to create mock phishing emails or webpages that are then sent to employees. These fake attacks help employees understand the different forms a phishing attack can take, identifying features, and to avoid clicking malicious links or leaking sensitive data in malicious forms.[71, 72]

11.4.10 Minimize use of personal devices or use of work devices for personal reasons

It is bad practice to allow staff to use personal equipment for accessing sensitive systems. Personal equipment may not be adequately secure and staff may leave the organization with sensitive data on their device. They may also share their devices with friends and family, potentially exposing sensitive data. It is equally bad practice to allow staff to use office equipment for personal reasons.

[71] Dashlane. 2020. *How to run an effective phishing test at work.* 7 March. https://blog.dashlane.com/phishing-test/

[72] Aidinyantz, N. 2017. *How to Run a Phishing Simulation Test: An Example from GlobalSign.* GlobalSign. https://www.globalsign.com/en/blog/how-to-run-a-simulated-phishing-test.

11.5 Pitfalls

11.5.1 Self-hosting security

A common misconception is that hosting sensitive data systems yourself or in-country is more secure than cloud-based systems that may be located on international servers. All systems require resources and maintenance and, therefore, it may be preferable have your system hosted and operated by a third-party provider with a track record of secure services, particularly if these skills and resources are not available locally.

11.5.2 Internet of Things may not be secure

It is becoming more common for medical devices to be connected to the internet for monitoring and automation, such as temperature for vaccines or vital signs data capturing. However, these devices are not necessarily secure and likely need configuration to set up security protocols. Furthermore, these insecure devices may be able to be accessed remotely, which then gives access to your entire network. Purchase devices from reputable sources and manufacturers and only connect them to your network if necessary. Where possible, ensure that the network is segmented to store sensitive data.

11.5.3 Occasionally connected systems

Managing data systems in an offline or occasionally connected environment can be challenging. In remote locations, it may not be practical for IT staff to service the site regularly. Therefore, a carefully planned and deliberate service schedule should be implemented with advanced communication to ensure that staff are prepared for site visits. Software updates can be downloaded on removable media to install during these visits to keep systems up-to-date. Secure off-site backup may be difficult for remote locations. If removable media is used for daily or weekly backups, ensure it is encrypted to mitigate the risk of data leaks through loss or theft.

11.5.4 Illegally obtained software

Malware is often distributed through downloaded pirated software. Attackers bundle malware with the application and distribute it through peer-to-peer files sharing applications or online storage sites. Often, pirated software cannot be updated, also making it vulnerable to attacks. Ensure that channels for purchasing legal software are set up through a central office or headquarters and distributed electronically within your organization.

11.5.5 Cloud-based backup considerations

When storing backup data in cloud-based systems, consider your process of uploading data. Products that synchronize a local folder with a cloud-based system, such as Dropbox, could be susceptible to data corruption in the event of ransomware on the system that stores and synchronizes the data. Files can become encrypted, making them inaccessible on the cloud-based system in that same format. Also, consider the legal implications around storing sensitive data. Are there legal restrictions on storing patient data on hardware systems outside your country, even if that information is encrypted? In some cases, an encrypted off-site backup may be your only option.

11.5.6 Mobile devices

Mobile devices, such as phones and tablets, are often used for field data entry and are particularly at risk if they are taken home with staff. Ensure that staff understand the conditions of use of mobile devices and ensure that are secured at all times, for example lock them away and do not share passwords. Use mobile device management (MDM) software to manage the device's access control features, software distribution, device location tracking, and even remote wiping in the event of a major security breach.

11.6 Quick tip

Test, test, test

Test data recovery processes periodically to ensure that backups are adequate and the process and system is functioning. Never assume that the recovery process will just work when required. Test the entire process from backup to restoration.

11.7 Practice spotlight

Data security and privacy in Tonga

In 2018, Tonga started to revive its digital health information system that links health facilities around the country and provides consistency in patient care wherever patients are located. A key requirement for the system is how it handles data security and privacy. Patient data needs to be confidential and safe but also available to appropriate clinicians to ensure health service delivery is the best it can be. Tonga recognized the need for a system that could provide a unique health identifier, clear user permissions, and well established and maintained role-based access. These permissions ensure that based on the role of the person accessing the system, they are able to see information relevant to their function. To support the use of the system and maintain the integrity of information, the system implementation was accompanied by training for all staff, from those admitting patients through to specialist doctors. The training focused on how to use the system and covered aspects on how the system uses passwords and audit logs to maintain confidentiality. This was in addition to basic IT computer training to managing/addressing any potential resistance from staff who are not computer literate. Policies to support the use of the system as well as a review of all relevant legislation and regulations will support users of the system. Tonga will also invest in implementing the policies with a clear plan on how they will be enforced to ensure maximum compliance. The knowledge provided through training and policies will also help health workers engage with patients on how their private information will be kept safe and confidential.

Dr Siale Akauola—CEO, Ministry of Health, Tonga

11.8 Resources and references

Standards and guidelines:

Reference: Pacific Islands Cyber Security Standards Cooperation Agenda. Standards Australia

Reference: Data Security and Confidentiality Guidelines for HIV, Viral Hepatitis, Sexually Transmitted Disease and Tuberculosis Programs. CDC. 2011.

Reference: Department of Homeland Security: IT Disaster Recovery plan template

Reference: mHealth Data Security, Privacy, and Confidentiality

Tools and frameworks:

Reference: The Privacy, Confidentiality and Security Assessment Tool (UNAIDS 2019)

Reference: National Institute of Standards and Technology (NIST). U.S. Department of Commerce. Governance framework

Training and certification:

Reference: International Organization for Standardization. ISO/IEC 27000 Information Security Management

Reference: Free security awareness training at Wizer.

Reference: Security training for IT professionals: Coursera.

Organizations and associations

Reference: The Pacific islands chapter of the Internet Society

Reference: Commonwealth Telecommunications Organisation: Cybersecurity

Reference: The Commonwealth Cyber Declaration Programme

12. INFRASTRUCTURE, DATA CENTER AND STORAGE

12.1 Overview

In Pacific island countries, there are two focuses to digital health infrastructure: establishing and strengthening the physical resources and hardware needed to communicate via the internet within a country and regionally, and secondly telecommunications infrastructure such as optical fiber lines, networks and satellites. Data centers with networking equipment, storage and servers are necessary components to meet the regional goal of providing Universal Health Coverage. Decisions made when designing digital health infrastructure have a far-reaching impact on resources and outcomes. Sound decisions made early on have the capacity to increase productivity, reduce wastage and improve overall security and uptime of digital health systems.

12.2 Goals to accomplish

To design and implement country-level infrastructure and facility-level data centers that are cost-effective, sustainable, secure, and meet the needs of the healthcare sector both centrally and remotely.

12.3 Importance

Why properly designed infrastructure, data center and storage are important

Planning an effective infrastructure reduces operating costs and enhances the sustainability of country-level and facility-level digital health systems. Systems should be designed according to resources and budgets to be maintainable over the life span of the system. Security is an important aspect of infrastructure planning and both physical and logical security needs to be sound to protect the privacy of clients and staff.

12.4 Best practices

12.4.1 Requirements assessment[73]

Conduct a thorough requirements assessment before building a data center or spending money on infrastructure. Solicit input from all stakeholders as required to understand and produce a system that meets the need. Involve individuals who have experience selecting and designing infrastructure projects, matching needs and budget. It's often difficult to get further investment funding or to make changes at infrastructure level once deployment has happened and so it's especially important to get the design "right" the first time out.

[73] Cisco. n.d. *What is a Data Center?* www.cisco.com/c/en/us/solutions/data-center-virtualization/what-is-a-data-center.html.

Figure 12. Questions to consider when planning infrastructure, data center and storage

QUESTIONS TO CONSIDER WHEN

PLANNING INFRASTRUCTURE, DATA CENTER AND STORAGE

NETWORK INFRASTRUCTURE

Is this a dedicated self-hosted system?

Can the system be hosted in a cloud warehouse?

Is this a co-location* environment?

*privately owned equipment hosted at a third-party data center

Is there sufficient cooling and power?

Will equipment be rack-mounted, freestanding or both?

How is security being handled? Are there firewalls set up?

What network cabling is required?

STORAGE INFRASTRUCTURE

Is Storage Area Network (SAN) or backup/tape storage available?

COMPUTING RESOURCES

What servers are already available?

What kind of data center management software is being used/available?

Adapted from *What is a Data Center?* www.cisco.com/c/en/us/solutions/data-center-virtualization/what-is-a-data-center.html.

12.4.2 Partner with other government departments

In most of the cases, network capacity within a government network is a major constraint and it is not feasible to upgrade network capacity solely under a digital health initiative. Partner with other government departments such as the education department and other ICT departments for setting standards, finding funding, and setting the implementation road map. Selecting solutions and prioritizing functionalities should be driven by current and future network capacity. Furthermore, network support mechanisms, monitoring, and maintenance should be the role of a centralized IT team, not the health department.

12.4.3 Establishing standards

Typically, a national health information system is the sum of government owned and curated equipment, software, and infrastructure and third-party (NGO, local partner) equipment, software, and infrastructure. Responsibilities for maintaining each system depends on the institution. While it may not be the role of government to enforce specific choices on partners, it is beneficial to have a minimum required standard for fundamental components, particularly for the security of infrastructure. Organizations such as the Pacific Islands Telecommunications Association have members that can share experiences and guide government ministries to set standards so that technology can be leveraged to the greatest extent.

12.4.4 Budget for ongoing maintenance and expansion

It is important to accurately account for capital expenditure and ongoing maintenance costs when designing infrastructure. Maintenance costs should include staffing, external support costs, servicing and replacement of equipment, and upgrading software licenses, etc.[74]

12.4.4 Design for scalability

Systems should be built with scalability in mind. Ensure that room for growth is factored into the budget and physical design without over-provisioning. Purchase servers and interconnecting equipment rated at higher specifications than required to start with, factoring in room for growth up to 5 years into the future.

Use high-grade cabling and connectivity components to ensure that future upgrades to network connectivity speeds do not require replacing cables and that downtime through component failure is minimal. Ensure space for growth beyond 5 years for the cabling system because upgrading is expensive.

Avoid common corner-cutting practices such as omitting patch panels in the design. Patch panels are an important component of a flexible network cable architecture and allow changes to routing and topology without having to disrupt the core network infrastructure. Conducting a thorough requirements assessment should allow for appropriate growth.

With the evolution from on-premises, self-hosted systems toward various service models such as Software as a Service (SaaS), Platform as a Service (PaaS), Infrastructure as a Service (IaaS), the choices and flexibility for building a modern digital health infrastructure are far greater today than in the past.[75]

12.4.6 Estimate power requirements

Account accurately for distribution of power to avoid overloading individual circuits. Power is an important factor in running a stable data center. Include redundant power supplies and uninterruptible power supply (UPS) units in the design not only for servers but also for adequate cooling. When purchasing UPS, plan for enough backup power to keep systems running, including cooling systems, through extended outages. Rural sites may benefit from alternate power sources such as solar and battery backup.

12.4.7 Estimate cooling requirements

Ensure that cooling is adequate. As systems become more powerful and as the data center grows, additional cooling to keep equipment running at optimal temperatures must be factored into growth plans. Ensure that systems concealed in cabinets have adequate heat dissipation. Even if the ambient temperature in the room is cool, with poor heat dissipation, server cabinets can get hot.

Ensure that LAN switching equipment supports Virtual LANs (VLANs) to segment traffic logically and mitigate the risk of malware distribution.

---

[74] ADB. 2018. *Guidance for Investing in Digital Health.* May. www.adb.org/publications/guidance-investing-digital-health.

[75] BMC Blogs. 2019. *SaaS vs PaaS vs IaaS: What's The Difference and How To Choose.* June. www.bmc.com/blogs/saas-vs-paas-vs-iaas-whats-the-difference-and-how-to-choose/.

12.4.8 Consider cloud hosting

Cloud service-based hosting models, as opposed to self-hosting, are often more affordable, are easier to plan and scale and require less maintenance. Cloud services can drive overall costs down and facilitate more accurate budgeting.

12.4.9 Ensure redundancy and disaster planning

Factor in as much redundancy into mission-critical systems as possible. Establish and document disaster recovery plans and policies. Based on the country and complexity of the hardware, document estimated and reasonable disaster recovery time frames—usually somewhere between hours to days. Factor in all threats when designing a data center including physical threats such as fire, theft, and flooding. Not all solutions are high-tech; consider whether simple, practical steps can mitigate risk, such as elevating equipment and cabling in areas prone to flooding.

12.4. 10 Document infrastructure components

The importance of documentation should not be understated. Infrastructure documentation includes diagrams, hardware and software inventory lists, and maintenance schedules. Accurate and up-to-date documentation saves time, effort, and money, particularly when vendors or new technical staff are required to work on systems. Proper documentation makes planning for future updates easier.

12.5 Pitfalls

12.5.1 Failing to accurately estimate maintenance costs

It is a common mistake to assume that IT systems are autonomous and need little to no maintenance after deployment. Often, capital expenditure is taken into account, but ongoing maintenance of the system is not planned or budgeted for. A common scenario is to deploy a central data center or remote installation without factoring in the additional effort required to maintain it or the cost of service contracts or warranties. The labor cost of regular maintenance, systems inspections and repairs and the cost of part replacement, need to be factored into the total cost of ownership.[76]

Maintenance costs for self-hosting servers can be challenging to estimate and mission-critical systems should have as much redundancy built in from the start to avoid downtime. Equally important is having a plan to cover the cost of a full replacement of core IT systems in case of a complete system failure.

12.5.2 Failing to accurately account for disaster recovery time frames

It is tempting to want to buy the most powerful system your budget can afford. Failure to factor in redundancy and support costs can be disastrous. Bear in mind that even if equipment is covered under warranty, it takes time to source and configure replacement equipment and restore the system to its former state after a disaster.

12.5.3 Failing to plan properly for cable management

Cable management is an often-overlooked discipline. All too often, rushed installation jobs result in maintenance problems. Poor cable management (labelling, mapping and documentation) leads to unnecessary outages and increases time wastage in ordinary maintenance.

12.6 Quick tip

Outside visitors to an office expect internet access or printer access. For office local area network (LAN), it is prudent to create a separate guest network, particularly over wifi. You have little or no control over equipment such as phones, tablets, or computers that belong to third parties and they could pose a threat if infected with malware.

[76] Data Foundry. 2019. *Estimating Data Center Cost of Ownership: 5 Hidden Costs.* August. www.datafoundry.com/blog/estimating-data-center-cost-ownership-5-hidden-costs.

12.7 Spotlight

Cook Islands digital transformation opportunity

In 2019, the Cook Islands reached a digital adoption crossroads. The small country, with an estimated population of 17,500, had seen a 52% increase in the number of internet users and a 100% increase in the number of mobile social media users from the previous year.[77] Furthermore, the laying of the Manatua international submarine cable connecting Rarotonga and Aitutaki was completed and went live in 2020, making high-bandwidth internet available and hopefully affordable. This cable presented an opportunity for both the government, as well as the private sector, to consider how best to meet the expected increased demand for digital services emanating from public services, businesses, and individual users. Additionally, the government proceeded to reform its telecommunications sector with the endorsement of the Telecommunications Market Competition Policy 2019, the introduction of the new Telecommunications Bill (now the Telecommunications Act 2019) and the enactment of the Competition and Regulatory Authority Act 2019 that allowed for the subsequent establishment and appointment of the Chairperson to the new Competition and Regulatory Authority. An opportunity to lead a significant digital transformation for the country had presented itself and the government was determined to embrace it.

Accordingly, and using best practices, the government engaged a strategic consulting firm to both develop a picture of the existing situation and make recommendations for substantially increasing both digital technologies and human resources within the Government of the Cook Islands.

Specializing in infrastructure development for internet, broadband, and mobile services, this consulting firm's infrastructure assessment highlighted a high risk of extended service disruption and an inadequate centralized data center. These infrastructure limitations were intensified by limited technical skills and human resource capacity within the country. Furthermore, a lack of ICT policies and procedures, planning, budgeting, and management of IT, hardware and software, business continuity created more risk for the system.[78] Major infrastructure failure could result in significant downtime and loss of critical data.

To address these limitations, the government recently embarked on a national approach to ICT, with a proposal to establish a Ministry of ICT. In essence this ministry would be responsible for setting strategy, policy and regulations for the country. Moreover, the ministry will also be responsible for delivering ICT to government agencies and citizens, driving government-wide use and adoption of ICT.

Currently, ICT sits within the Office of the Prime Minister as a division responsible for maintaining the Government ICT network and providing end-user support to government employees.

Recently, the ICT Division proceeded through the government's tender process to secure a private company to undertake a major infrastructure project that will include the upgrade of the government's ICT network and the establishment of a co-location for the Cook Islands Government Data Center. The Data Center is expected to meet the minimum specifications required to provide 24/7 operation and to be established in-country. In parallel, there will be commitment toward a complete documentation of the government's ICT systems, development of policies, procedures and inter-agency service level agreements.

Public health was identified as one of the sectors that was most e-ready and would immediately benefit from the infrastructure upgrade and co-location services. The Cook Islands requires that patient and other citizen data resides in-country for the time being. The upgraded and secure centralized government network is anticipated to significantly improve government inter-agency processes and to better serve the public by making its services available online.

Although progress presents challenges, it also provides for opportunities and scope for improvement, growth, and innovation.

Pua Hunter
Director of ICT, Office of the Prime Minister
Government of the Cook Islands

[77] Kitskoo. 2019. *Government of the Cook Islands eGovernment Assessment & Recommendation presentation,* May.

[78] Kitskoo. 2019. *e-Government Assessment & Recommendation for The Cook Islands,* April.

13. RISK MANAGEMENT

13.1 Overview

Digital health systems are inherently complex, involve a wide set of stakeholders, impact existing healthcare delivery processes, and often require an entirely new skill set for technology and healthcare staff. These and other project aspects and dynamics bring a level of uncertainty or risk, which can have positive or negative effects on a project.[79] Risk management should identify, quantify, monitor, and implement risk responses in an intentional and controlled way, to maximize opportunities and minimize negative consequences.

13.2 Goals to accomplish

The risk management goal is to create a plan for handling risk events, should they materialize. The process of identifying possible project issues—from implementing new technologies where team experience can be minimal to managing stakeholders' expectations—helps to align scope, scheduling, communication, and funding resources and mitigate potential problems. Part of risk management is the ongoing monitoring and mitigation of known risks, while being alert to new risks.

13.3 Importance

Why risk management is important

Risk management in digital health projects is necessary to mitigate major project failure, avoid rework, focus and balance effort, as well as stimulate win–win outcomes. Digital health projects often require organizational and process changes that may impact business objectives and success.[80] Project risks will be specific to your digital health implementation and may include the following risk areas and types.[81]

Table 8. Possible risk areas and types to be managed

Risk area	Potential types of risk	
Technology	• Usability/ease of use of the software or system • Interoperability of technology components • Technology infrastructure	• System architecture • Reliability and stability of communications structures • Conforming to hardware or software standards
System management and adoption	• Governance and policies • Availability of funding, initial and ongoing • Training for clinicians; training for ICT professionals • Impact on healthcare quality	• Patient or clinician safety • Clinician buy-in • Patient privacy and security • Culture and hidden gender bias
Project management	• Cost overruns • Schedule delays	• Scope creep • Leadership definite

79 Project Management Institute. 2017. *A guide to the project management body of knowledge* (PMBOK GUIDE). Sixth edition.

80 Conceição Granja, C. Janssen, W., Johansen, M.A. 2018. 'Factors Determining the Success and Failure of eHealth Interventions: Systematic Review of the Literature', *Journal of Medical Internet Research*. May. www.ncbi.nlm.nih.gov/pmc/articles/PMC5954232/.

81 Conceição Granja, C. Janssen, W., Johansen, M.A. 2018. 'Factors Determining the Success and Failure of eHealth Interventions: Systematic Review of the Literature', *Journal of Medical Internet Research*. May. www.ncbi.nlm.nih.gov/pmc/articles/PMC5954232/.

13.4 Best practice

13.4.1 Create a risk management plan

Risk management plans include the following steps (see footnote 81). The most important steps are to identify the risks, discuss and document mitigation strategies and frequently monitor the risks. The process of quantifying risk impact will help stakeholders determine how much effort is required to mitigate the risk or re-think the technology approach.

Figure 13. How to create a risk management plan

HOW TO CREATE A
RISK MANAGEMENT PLAN
1
IDENTIFY
2
QUALIFY
3
QUANTIFY
4
PLAN
5
IMPLEMENT
6
MONITOR
1. Identify risks: Identify individual project risks as well as sources of overall project risk and document their characteristics. This is a very important step in the process and should produce a comprehensive list of any barriers to success of the digital health implementation and adoption. This step can be done with the help of a risk register, a simple tool where risks are organized and documented.
2. Perform qualitative risk analysis: Describe the risk characteristics and determine the probability and impact of the risk. If you are not sure of the probably of occurrence, assign a high, medium or low impact based on experience. This kind of analysis tends to be subjective in nature but quick to perform.
3. Perform quantitative risk analysis: Numerically analyse the probable and impact of a risk event using quantitative or statistical methods. This kind of analysis is much more difficult to perform because it involves knowing actual or close numeric estimates of probability and impact. This kind of analysis take more time to do, is more detailed but is more objective than qualitative risk analysis.
4. Plan risk responses: Develop options, select strategies and agree on actions to address overall project risk exposure, as well to treat individual project risks.
5. Implement risk responses: Implement agreed-on risk plans.
6. Monitor risks: Monitor the implementation of risk response plans, tracking identified risks, identifying and analysing new risks, and evaluating the effectiveness of risk processes throughout the project.

Table 9. **Risk register example (qualitative risk analysis)**

Risk type	Description	Probability	Impact	Mitigation strategy	Date last reviewed
Data entry forms/ mobile application	The mobile implementation will not meet expectations; the features may not meet needs.	.25	Medium	Do pilot testing and find out issues Mitigate by doing demos/ UAT to review forms	31 May 2019

13.4.2 Identify and include a "business champion" as part of the project leadership team

It is important to identify a business champion as part of the project leadership. By including business champions in the project team, business objectives, and processes can be aligned with the digital health project objectives and scope, setting stakeholder expectations and reducing the risk of project failure. Establish a close operating relationship between the business owner and the IT project manager so that they can work through issues and make optimal decisions for the project.

13.4.3 Create a risk-aware culture

The project manager is not the only person responsible for tracking, monitoring and mitigating risks. Everyone in the team is responsible for risk management which includes identifying and reporting issues. Stakeholders should be included in risk register reviews and encouraged to identify emerging risks throughout the course of the project.

13.4.4 Use an agile project management approach

Use an "agile" approach to manage digital health projects as guided by, for example, the Agile Manifesto,[82] which embraces the concept of change and provides simple guidelines that can help reduce risk. These guidelines emphasize:

- interacting with people for optimal innovation and output
- prioritizing project activities to maximize business value
- splitting up project activities into short time frames
- allowing for interim quality and functional validation.

13.5 Pitfalls

Research shows that planning, monitoring, and applying corrective actions to risk management is difficult.[83] Some pitfalls that should be avoided when undertaking risk management activities include:

- failing to refer to your risk management plan during the course of the project
- overstating the benefit of a project and understating the risks or uncertainties, leading to inflated expectations of the project's deliverables
- not applying lessons learned from previous projects in terms of costs, time and skills required
- downplaying or ignoring the characteristics and behavior of individual project stakeholders.

13.6 Quick tip

Routinely review a risk register

Integrate a risk register into your weekly or monthly project reporting so that risk management and monitoring become part of your routine project management activities.

[82] Manifesto for Agile Software Development, https://agilemanifesto.org/

[83] De Bakker, K., Boonstra, A., and Wortmann, H. (2010). 'Does risk management contribute to IT project success? A meta-analysis of empirical evidence', *International Journal of Project Management*, University of Groningen, The Netherlands.

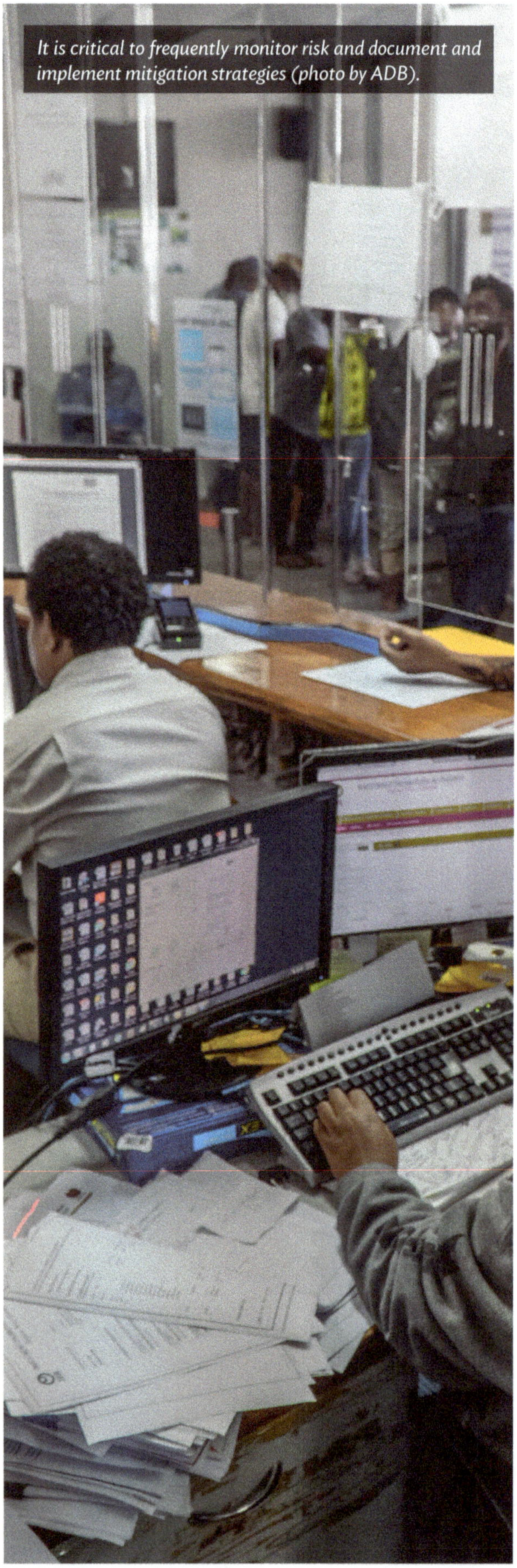

It is critical to frequently monitor risk and document and implement mitigation strategies (photo by ADB).

13.7 Practice spotlight

Cook Islands Risk Management

Collaboration and sharing our experience and knowledge with other countries, government departments and working groups has had a direct and positive impact on lowering our implementation risk. With the Cook Islands health system transitioning to a new patient information management system (PIMS), our ICT team's approach to the procurement process and migration of data has relied heavily on our collaboration with relevant international and local partners and experts. This has included working with the Cook Islands Ministry of Education who has experience in implementing IT systems in the Cook Islands' environment, as well as a primary health organization in New Zealand to gain insight into their procurement and phased implementation process for their PIMS. Both organizations generously shared information about infrastructure, software and vendors, as well as their procurement and project management processes. This collaboration helped save time and reduce risk, and assisted in the refining of our PIMS specifications.

Daphne Ringi
Director—Planning and Funding
Te Marae Ora—Ministry of Health

13.8 Resources and references

- ***Resource:*** Risk management register This risk register is a template to record all risks identified during the project planning stage of the project. Use it to monitor and document emerging risks through the life of your digital health project. The register template is for the qualitative estimation of probability and impact of identified risks.

14. PATIENT PORTALS

14.1 Overview

A natural extension of an electronic medical records (EMR) system or other digital health system is the ability for patients to access their health records, online through a patient portal.

> *"A patient portal is a secure online website that give patients convenient, 24-hour access to personal health information from anywhere with an internet connection."*[84]

In addition to giving access to health documents such as doctors' notes, lab results, and prescriptions, patient portals should provide a secure communication channel for clinicians. Administrative tasks such as making appointments and paying bills may also be included in a patient portal.

With the promise of an enhanced quality of care comes the responsibility of the portal provider to provide security, privacy, and confidentiality of patient data as well as user support, adoption, and use.

14.2 Goals to accomplish

To understand the needs of the patient population and match them to the available patient data and system features that are already available as part of an EMR/EHR system or may be built to supplement the software. The ability to use and the adoption level of a patient portal is influenced by personal factors such as age, ethnicity, education level, health literacy, health status, and role as a caregiver.[85] Across the Pacific, women have less access to digital technology and the internet, compared to men. Implementing a patient portal should take this gender gap into account, as well as usability for people with disability and older people. In addition to the patient's needs, it is important to gather requirements for all stakeholders, including clinicians and supporting staff. As part of the planning for the implementation of a patient portal, processes must be put into place to notify, register and educate patients as well as to train staff on the ongoing management and support of the portal.

14.3 Importance

Why are patient portals important

Patient portals provide benefits to both patients and providers. Demonstrated benefits of patient portals include enhanced patient-provider communication, improved adherence to medication and discovery of medical errors. [86] Additionally, the convenience of making appointments online and viewing medical documentation such as lab results enhance the patient experience and patient satisfaction. Providers also benefit from less time spent on data entry for filling out registration or medical history forms that patients fill out themselves, with less time spent on the phone setting up appointments or answering questions leading to a reduction in required staff.[87]

14.4 Best practices

14.4.1 Work toward making patient portals part of the national digital health strategy

Patients are requesting to see and manage their healthcare data as well as to have greater access to providers. Providers, on the other hand, may be reticent in providing access to patient portals due to the added costs of the technology, changes to workflow, and data management risks. By including patient portals as part of a digital health strategy

84 HealthIT.gov. n.d. *What is a patient portal?* www.healthit.gov/faq/what-patient-portal.

85 Irizarry, T., DeVito Dabbs, A., & Curran, C. R. 2015. Patient Portals and Patient Engagement: A State of the Science Review. *Journal of Medical Internet Research*. 17(6). e148. https://doi.org/10.2196/jmir.4255.

86 Dendere, R., Slade, C., Burton-Jones, A., Sullivan, C., Staib, A., & Janda, M. 2019. Patient Portals Facilitating Engagement With Inpatient Electronic Medical Records: A Systematic Review. *Journal of Medical Internet Research*. 21(4). e12779. https://doi.org/10.2196/12779.

87 Burling-Phillips, L. 2013. *Patient Portals, Part 1: First Steps for Your Practice*, American Academy of Ophthalmology. December. www.aao.org/eyenet/article/patient-portals-part-1-first-steps-your-practice-2.

with clear steps to reaching this goal, organizations will be more likely to embrace this new digital health component.

14.4.2 *Provide a mobile version*

With increasing use of mobile internet and social media services and a steady reduction in costs,[88] taking a mobile-first approach has the potential for widespread adoption of patient portals. Development efforts should be focused to first work well on a smartphone or other mobile device and then in a PC format, with the anticipation that patients are more likely to use phones to access their healthcare information.

14.4.3 *Usability is critical*

Whether on a mobile device or a PC, a user-centric design is a key requirement. Careful attention is needed to make sure that the application is intuitive, allows for easy registration and login, does not use medical jargon, and is clearly labelled. Engage a user-experience professional to help design the user interface, using participatory principles that include women and girls. Ensure there are no constraints for access and use for people with disabilities, women, or vulnerable groups.

14.4.4. *Minimum feature set*

Consider this minimum feature set for a robust patient portal:[89]

- clinical summaries
- secure messaging
- online bill pay
- new patient registration
- ability to update demographic information
- prescription renewals and contact lens ordering
- appointment requests
- appointment reminders
- medication lists
- lab and test results
- medical history
- patient educational materials.

14.4.5 *Promote your portal to patients across all communication channels*

Patients who are occasional users or people who are typically healthy and do not visit the doctor or hospital regularly, need to be encouraged to use patient portals. Promote the portal's benefits to drive adoption. Consider marketing ideas such as posters in health facilities and in treatment rooms, providing brochures and adding a call out with the portal link address on billing statements and appointment cards. Also consider working with women's or disability groups to promote the portal and provide assistance to new users. Consider linking your portal with relevant hospitals in countries that provide tertiary care to your population.

14.5 Pitfalls

14.5.1 *Help patients understand the information provided*

It is easy to think about a patient portal as a technology solution by simply providing patient data, lab results, and medications. However, patients' health literacy may vary greatly and it is important to clearly explain the information provided and what to do next—for example, if a lab result is within standard range and, if not, the recommended next action. Furthermore, include trusted educational materials about diagnoses and treatment plans as a portal feature.

14.5.2 *Train facility staff on portal features from the patient's perspective*

It is important to train staff on both what patients can see and do on the portal, as well as what only facility staff can see and do on the portal. Patients who may not be familiar with using technology may feel intimidated and may be resistant to using the portal. To encourage adoption, provide training for patients, spouses or other caregivers on how to access and use the portal features.

[88] GSMA. 2019. The State of Mobile Internet Connectivity. www.gsma.com/mobilefordevelopment/wp-content/uploads/2019/07/GSMA-State-of-Mobile-Internet-Connectivity-Report-2019.pdf.

[89] Burling-Phillips, L. 2014. Patient Portals, Part 2: What Features Do You Need? American Academy of Ophthalmology, January, www.aao.org/eyenet/article/patient-portals-part-2-what-features-do-you-need.

14.5.3 Provide clinicians with a good user interface between the patient portal and electronic medical record

Some clinicians may be concerned about how increased communications through the portal's secure messaging will impact their daily workload and increased expectations that clinicians will promptly answer questions from patients.[90] Poor interfaces with EMRs can be a barrier to providing accurate information, requiring clinicians to search for information about patients, which is time consuming and, in many cases, not paid for by the patient or insurance.

14.5.4 Ask for patient feedback

It is important to engage patients and obtain feedback about the patient portal. Like any technology implementation, not every feature will used as expected. Issues can vary from difficulties logging in to seeing incorrect health data. Issues need to be addressed so that the portal works well and is adopted as desired. Ensure you are soliciting feedback from a diverse population, including women, people with disabilities, and vulnerable groups so the portal will suit different users' needs.

14.6 Quick tip

Patient data privacy is one of the key barriers of adopting patient portals. Apply the same security, privacy, and confidentiality policies and processes that are used for an organization's EMR such as requiring patient consent, strong passwords, providing a two-factor authentication option, encrypted data transfer, audit trails, and inform patients that the portal is a secure extension of their medical record.

14.7 Practice spotlight

Cook Islands Patient Portals

Te Marae Ora Cook Islands Ministry of Health is upgrading its patient information management system (PIMS). The PIMS was introduced in 2004 and operational across the whole of the Cook Islands. A key consideration for the new system is the patient portal which will allow patients (and health providers) to access accurate and complete patient information using health information platforms and portals via data exchange. The patient portal embraces progressive health technology improvements that seek to empower both patients and healthcare workers to access information for decision-making. Furthermore, the portal is intended to ensure transparency of healthcare protocols for both patients and providers, the standardization of data, and the quality and accuracy of information. The Cook Islands envisions an integrated digital health system, and the patient portal will be an essential component of the system. Improvements in infrastructure, governance, and overall software systems are driving integration and better reporting, which ultimately supports universal health coverage. The geographical nature of our region demands that we provide transportable data for optimal treatment and better population health outcomes.

Daphne Ringi

Director—Planning and Funding

Te Marae Ora—Ministry of Health

14.8 Resources and references

Reference: What is a patient portal?

Reference: Patient portal work plan

90 Miller, D. P., Jr, Latulipe, C., Melius, K. A., Quandt, S. A., & Arcury, T. A. 2016. Primary Care Providers' Views of Patient Portals: Interview Study of Perceived Benefits and Consequences. *Journal of Medical Internet Research*, 18(1), e8. https://doi.org/10.2196/jmir.4953.

When staff understand why data is collected and how the analysis of data can have a positive impact on healthcare programs, a data use and analytics program will be successful (photo by ADB).

ANALYTICS AND INNOVATION

ANALYTICS AND INNOVATION

CONTENTS

15 *Data use and analytics* **P72**

Data use and analytics is the process of collecting quality data and transforming it into information through aggregations, calculations, and visualizations so that it can be used for evidence-based decision-making.

Data use and analytics is an ongoing process for continual improvement of programs. When staff understand why data is being collected and how the analysis of data can have a positive impact on healthcare programs, a data use and analytics program will be successful.

- **Spotlight:** Monitoring of cold chain for vaccines—a pilot project in Vanuatu and Solomon Islands
- Data Demand and Use Concepts and Tools: A Training Tool Kit (Measure Evaluation)
- Data Quality Review Toolkit (World Health Organization)
- Data Viz Checklist (Stephanie Evergreen and Ann Emery)
- User Stories Indicator and Data Dictionary Template
- Steps to establish a data use and analytics program
- Developing a problem statement
- Roles and responsibility matrix for data use and quality
- Visualizations Business Rules Template

16 *Healthcare innovation* **P78**

Digital health innovation optimizes the performance and improves scalability of digital health systems to meet the digital health needs of a country or organization.

- **Spotlight:** Delivery of vaccines by drones in Vanuatu
- Digital Health Innovation: A Toolkit to Navigate From Concept to Clinical Testing
- Australian Government: Public Sector Innovation Network
- Working innovatively: A toolkit to support the use of innovative technology in practice
- Creating an innovation center of excellence
- The 7 Things Every Innovation Center Should Have
- Free software tool the help guide and manage the collection, evaluation and prioritization of ideas
- Public Health Innovations for COVID-19: Findings, Trusting and Scaling Innovation

15. DATA USE AND ANALYTICS

15.1 Overview

Data use and analytics for evidence-based decision-making is a key goal for all Pacific island countries.[91] The process entails collecting quality data and transforming it into information through aggregations, calculations, and visualizations at the facility, regional, and country level and making it available to different roles for their individual decision-making needs. Data use and analytics is an ongoing activity, with the goal of continual improvement of programs such as the monitoring of non-communicable diseases (NCD), a leading cause of premature death and disability in the Pacific.[92] Data use and analytics requires establishing realistic and sustainable data collection and reporting processes supported by paper-based and digital analytics tools. At a country-level, monitoring data such as mortality, morbidity, risk factors, and health system responses result in a better understanding of how to best treat patients for better outcomes. When staff members at all levels of the health system understand why data is being collected and how the analysis of the data can have a positive and lasting impact on a healthcare programs, a data use and analytics program will be successful.

Figure 14. Data informed decision-making cycle

DATA INFORMED DECISION-MAKING CYCLE

- Patient level data from electronic health records
- Community and other sources of data

COLLECT DATA

TRANSFORM & DISPLAY

- Aggregate
- Calculate indicators
- Display in reports and dashboards

MAKE DECISIONS

ANALYZE

- Changes in clinical approach
- Changes in program management
- Optimization of resources

- Outcomes versus targets
- Trends
- Outliers

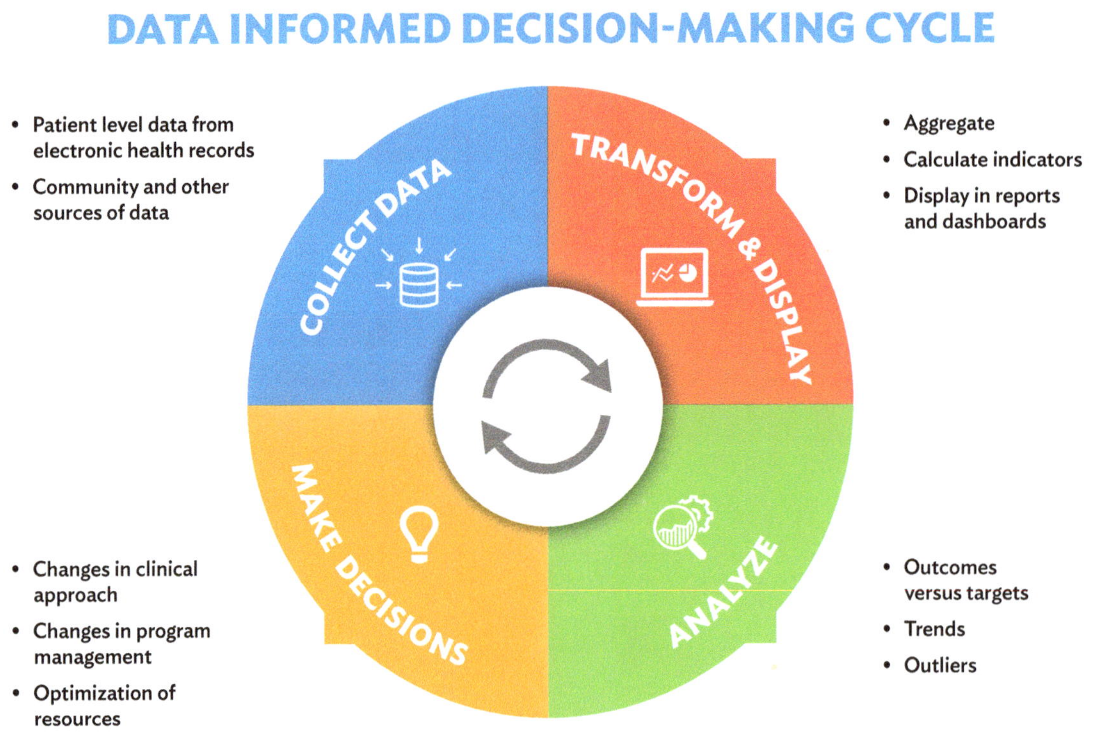

91 WHO, 2017. *Health Information Systems in the Pacific at a Glance 2016*. https://apps.who.int/iris/rest/bitstreams/1147902/retrieve.

92 Tolley, H. Snowdon, W., Wate, J., Durand, A.M., Vivili, P., McCool1, J., Novotny, R., Dewes, O., Hoy, D., Bell, C., Richards, N., and Swinburn, B. 2016. Monitoring and accountability for the Pacific response to the non-communicable diseases crisis. BMC Public Health. 16:958, DOI 10.1186/s12889-016-3614-8. www.ncbi.nlm.nih.gov/pmc/articles/PMC5018177/pdf/12889_2016_Article_3614.pdf.

15.2 Goals to accomplish

Significant program and policy decisions are frequently made based on insufficient data, even when there is abundant data from multiple sources.[93] Two important goals are required for successful data quality initiatives. The first is creating a culture of data use where staff are demanding data for evidence-based decisions. The second is consistently following the process of identifying available data, verifying the quality of the available data, cleaning and transforming the data, and establishing routine data analysis to create a continuous cycle of improvement and adaptive management.

15.3 Importance

Why data use and analytics are important

Healthcare providers and managers want to collect a lot of data with the hope that they will be able to form a full picture of a patient's medical situation or how a population of patients is trending in a disease area. But it is not enough to collect data and generate simple counts of data elements. For example, the count of women who visited an antenatal clinic does not say as much as comparing the count to a target or seeing the count plotted over time. With data transformations, information can be used to identify trends, measure, and find relationships that lead to insights and can assist in decision-making. This requires a culture of data demand and use and one that promotes a high quality of care, which reviews data to make decisions and constantly improves the health services and healthcare management processes. At each healthcare service level and facility level, regular reviews of the data collected and its analysis should be practiced.

Figure 15. Example of data visualization

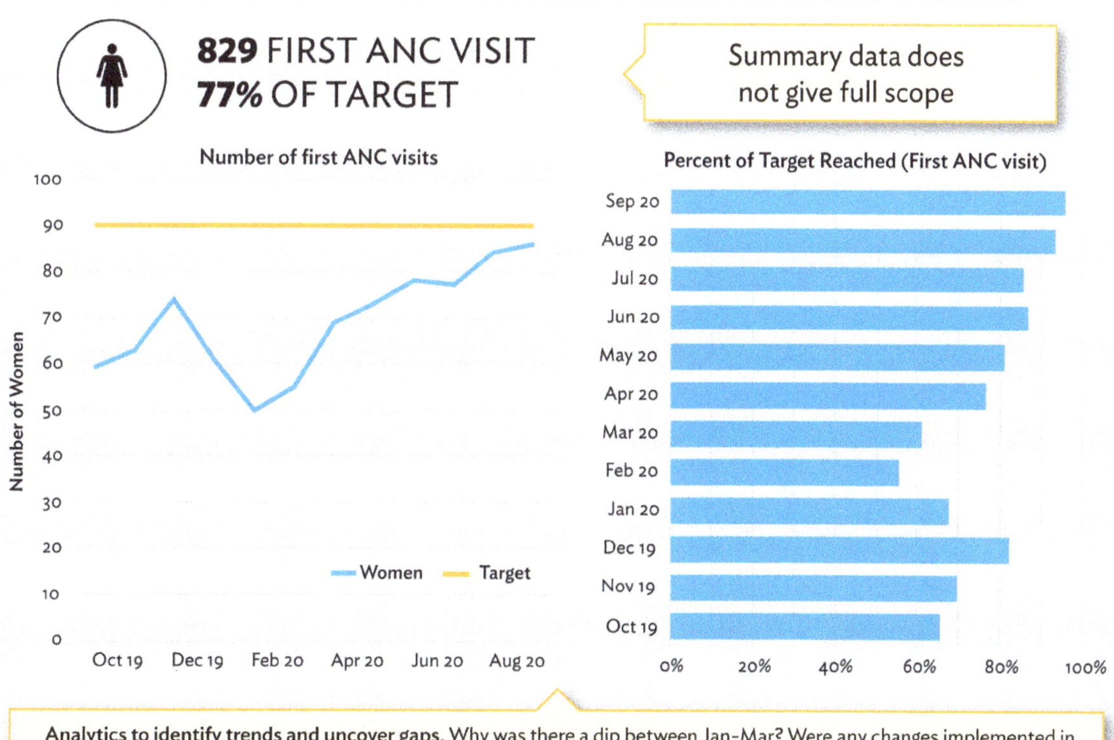

[93] MEASURE Evaluation Project 2011. Tools for Data Demand and Use in the Health Sector—Framework for Linking Data with Action. *Measure Evaluation Manual.* ms-11-46b, April. www.measureevaluation.org/resources/publications/ms-11-46-b.

15.4 Best practice

The key factors to promoting data use and analytics are as follows:

- make sure the system is collecting quality data for relevant indicators
- provide simple tools to report and visualize the data
- actively drive decision-making using the data and create a feedback loop so that staff collecting the data are also involved with the analysis and decisions made as a result of their efforts.

15.4.1 *Data quality for relevant indicators*

An effective data use and analytics program starts with collecting high-quality data at the patient or facility level. High-quality data is data that can be used with trust for decision-making, meaning that the data is accurate, reliable, precise, complete, collected in a timely manner, and is recorded in a consistent format and confidential way.[94] Collecting data that comprises all these attributes is difficult to consistently achieve and requires dedicated personnel and processes to oversee and monitor the collection activities. As part of a data-use initiative, the first step is to assess the data-capture tools and current processes, as well as to conduct an audit of the quality of the existing data.[95]

15.4.2 *Data management, analytics and visualization tools*

Digital data-capture tools and applications, such as databases, statistical and other transformative tools, as well as reporting and visualization tools are readily available. These tools help to uncover relationships between treatment and outcomes as well as show where overlap and gaps exist at the patient and program levels.

When selecting tools, it is important to consider the role and needs of users and their ability to integrate tools into routine work practices. Key factors that contribute successfully to adopting a data collection and reporting or visualization system are usability—the perceived ease of use and utility—and functional effectiveness.[96] A participatory approach to designing any system will assure buy-in from stakeholders and help to capture needs of men and women at all levels. Providing management support and ongoing user training is essential to the success of the data use and analytics program. Ongoing funding for maintenance and enhancement of the tool and software, data sharing across organizations and departments, and data security and confidentiality should all be considered to ensure widespread adoption of data collection and analytics tools.

15.4.3 *Data analytics training*

Adequate and ongoing training for users of reports and visualizations will improve adoption and minimize the risk of misinterpretation of results. Training may include interpreting and developing data visualizations, epidemiological modelling, GIS analysis, cluster analysis, and statistical modelling (refer to footnote 96). Training should target different roles in the healthcare delivery system and may be hands-on, self-paced tutorials, or through user guides. The skill levels of healthcare workers, administrators or leaders should be considered when developing the training curriculum and goals. Promoting the routine use of tools, visualizations, and analyses in daily functions and meetings will help users gain expertise and confidence in using information for decision-making.

15.4.4 *Linking data with decision-making processes*

Systems may already be collecting good-quality data, but it may not be used effectively for decision-making. Fundamentally, there must be a demand for data. This means that stakeholders and decision makers need to be motivated to use the available data and place value on the data being collected. To institutionalize data use, it is helpful to set up a framework that links questions or problems to data findings and recommendations for action. As part of this framework, communication channels should be established with decision makers and data-supported results can be shared within a prescribed timeline.[97] An example where data collection and dashboards are used extensively is in District Health Information Software 2 (DHIS2), an open source, web-based health management information system (HMIS) platform.

94 Hardee, K., 2008. Data Quality Audit Tool, Guidelines for Implementation, MEASURE Evaluation Project. MS-08-29 September.

95 WHO. 2017. Data Quality Review, Modules 1-3.

96 Carroll, L.N., Au, A.P., Detwiler, L.T., Fu, T., Painter, I.S., and Abernethy, N.F. 2014. Visualization and analytics tools for infectious disease epidemiology: A systematic review'. Journal of Biomedical Informatics. 51. pp. 287–298.

97 MEASURE Evaluation Project, 2011. Tools for Data Demand and Use in the Health Sector, Framework for Linking Data with Action. Measure Evaluation Manual. www.measureevaluation.org/resources/publications/ms-11-46-b.

Figure 16. Example of data dashboard from District Health Information Software 2 (DHIS2)

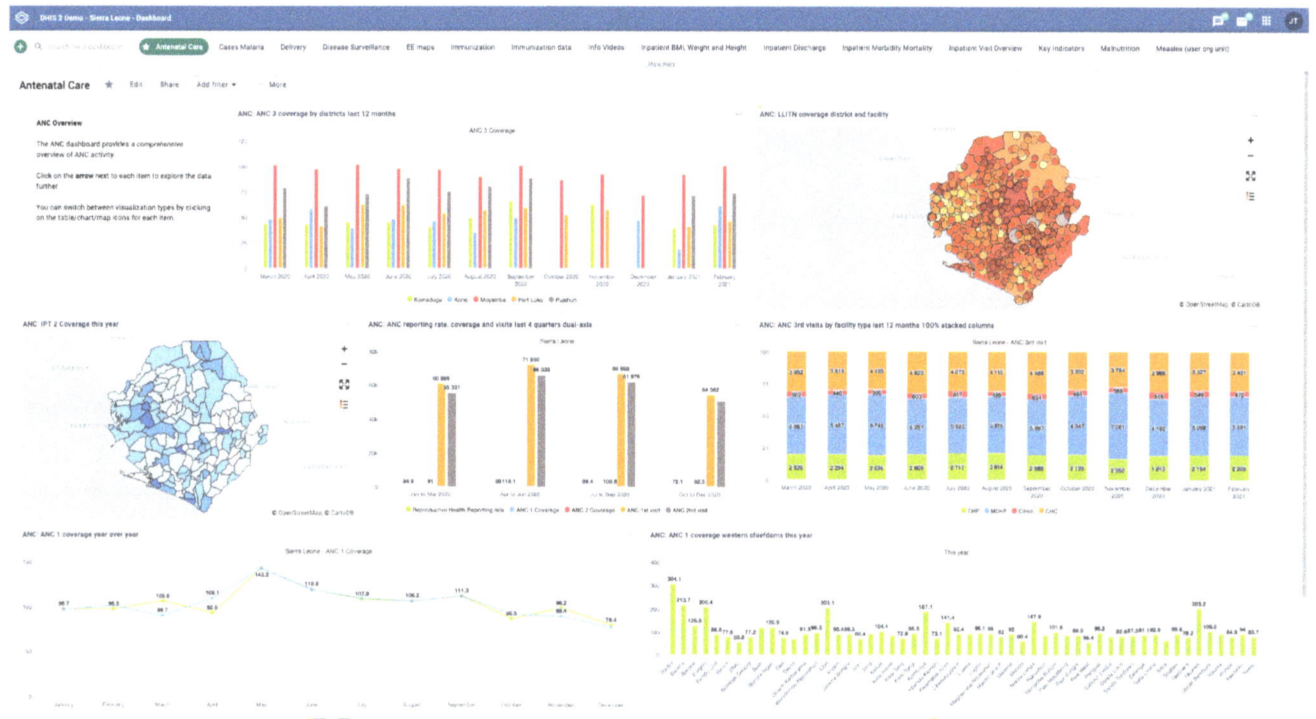

This platform is used by more than 70 low- and middle-income countries. The screenshot from their demonstration site shows graphs and maps, highlighting key indicators and other metrics. This central dashboard can be used by leaders and decision makers regularly to monitor indicators leading to informed program changes for improved outcomes.

15.4.5 Establish a personal health information protection policy

Patient data confidentiality and security of identifiable data must be addressed as part of a data use and analytics program. It is easy to forget that patient data continues to be confidential, even when working with it internally. Policies around how to handle lists of patient data with patient names or screen shots that end up in presentations must be documented and followed. Three related concepts affect the protection of data: privacy, confidentiality, and security and outlined fully in Chapter 11.

15.5 Pitfalls

15.5.1 Do not expect skills and process changes to take hold quickly

Developing a culture of data use and analytics for decision-making involves a lot of people in different roles and with different skills, from the facility level up to the Ministry of Health to the statistics department overseeing the collection of birth and deaths information.

It is easy to become overwhelmed with all the facets required of data: from verifying data quality through to data warehouses and creating dashboards. Identify a champion at each level in the reporting hierarchy, led by the Ministry of Health, and focus on one high-priority healthcare area to start. Bring together a working group to set direction and pilot a data-use initiative in a handful of facilities.

15.5.2 Do not make data quality all about reporting up

Many data collection initiatives are driven by donor requirements. Often, staff at facilities are not included in the routine analysis of results. Data use will become part a facility's culture if there is a well-established and continual feedback loop where facility staff can see results and make local program adjustments.

15.5.3 Use sustainable and accessible data visualization tools

A range of reporting and dashboard software tools and packages are available for purchase, but many require licensing. Make sure that ongoing funding is available for the tools you select for all staff levels before you invest in the development and training of the report production or visualization. Ensure tools provide options for accessibility for people with disabilities.

15.5.4 Understand national policies about personal data security

If personal identifiable information cannot leave the facility and because digital tools allow individuals to view data remotely, understanding and establishing strict access rights and restricting access to patient-level and line-level reports must be established as part of all data use and visualization initiatives. Furthermore, determining where patient-level data will be stored, whether on-premises or in-the-cloud, in-country or out-of-country, can have a significant impact on system requirements, staff to manage the technology and funding needs to maintain the system.

15.6 Quick tip

Work backward from the reports or visualizations you want to create and verify that your organization is collecting the right indicators to answer the questions you are asking. If you are not collecting the right indicators, determine a proxy indicator with the understanding the results may be higher or lower than if the correct indicator was collected.

15.7 Practice spotlight

Monitoring of cold chain for vaccines—a pilot project in Vanuatu and Solomon Islands

Vaccination coverage for infants and children in the Pacific island countries is particularly challenging because of the difficult terrain and issues with vaccine supply. Mothers and children may need to travel long distances on foot and by boat to reach a health clinic. These long journeys may also introduce other hardships such as leaving children unattended at home or leaving household-sustaining work. Unfortunately, it is not uncommon for vaccines to be out of stock or even spoiled due to refrigeration failure at clinics, resulting in an unsuccessful health clinic visit. These failures delay vaccine schedules, putting children and vulnerable populations at risk for contracting diseases.

Innovative technologies and data use have been applied to the vaccine supply chain to address the need for a temperature-controlled environment for vaccines, called a cold chain. The cold chain begins with cold storage at the manufacturing plant, during transport and delivery and then at the health clinic, finally ending with the administration of the vaccine to the patient. Vaccine temperature should be maintained between 2 °C and 8 °C, otherwise potency may be lost or completely destroyed.[98]

At the health clinic, monitoring and maintaining the vaccine cold chain requires individual health workers to remember to check stock levels and record temperatures regularly, taking the health worker away from primary care duties. Paper-based systems are the traditional method for recording the data, which is then relayed to a central unit for supply management and refrigeration maintenance. This data collection process is critical for the success of any vaccine program and it is important that the data is accurate, reliable, precise, and complete. With the use of technology, the data collection process can be made much easier producing more and better data for decision-making.

A pilot project in Vanuatu and Solomon Islands deployed Bluetooth technology to monitor refrigerator temperatures and vaccine stock. Data is collected on a prescribed schedule, which is automatically synched to a mobile device when the device is within range of the refrigerator.

98 Center for Disease Control. 2015. Vaccine Storage and Handling Toolkit. April. https://www.cdc.gov/vaccines/hcp/admin/storage/toolkit/storage-handling-toolkit.pdf

This data is then sent to a central database via the internet. Data indicators measure vaccine availability, refrigerator temperatures and temperature breaches, providing health managers with a bird's-eye view of vaccine stock levels as well as informing maintenance and replacement schedules for refrigerators.

For women taking children for vaccines, the Bluetooth technology promises no more wasted journeys or gaps in vaccination schedules. For health practitioners, the technology reduces the administration burden leading to greater efficiencies in supply chains and refrigerator maintenance.

15.8 Resources and references

What's your question and how do you measure it?

These resources cover how to assess data quality, establish or improve data use in your organization, and how-to develop understandable and readable data visualizations.

Reference: Data Demand and Use Concepts and Tools: A Training Tool Kit (Measure Evaluation) A multi-module training tool kit that covers aspects of data use for decision-making within and organization or program.

Reference: Data Quality Review Toolkit (World Health Organization) A framework and toolkit for assessing the quality of data generated by information systems based in health facilities.

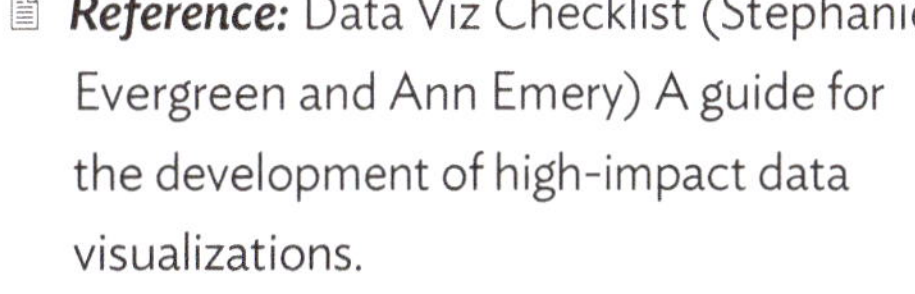

Reference: Data Viz Checklist (Stephanie Evergreen and Ann Emery) A guide for the development of high-impact data visualizations.

Resource: User Stories Indicator and Data Dictionary Template

Resource: Steps to establish a data use and analytics program

Resource: Developing a problem statement

Resource: Roles and responsibility matrix for data use and quality

Resource: Visualization business rules

16. HEALTHCARE INNOVATION

16.1 Overview

Innovative healthcare delivery approaches are needed to overcome the challenges of geography, human resources, and funding resources prevalent in the Pacific island region. Digital health technologies can take advantage of broadband and internet connectivity, telemedicine, mobile phones, and even the use of drones. Establishing and embracing an innovative culture at the country and facility levels where organizations and individuals are encouraged to suggest new ideas, test them and then optimize them, has long-term pay-offs.[99]

> *"Health innovation identifies new or improved health policies, systems, products and technologies, and services and delivery methods that improve people's health and wellbeing."*[100]

Innovation does not have to cost a lot and can start locally. With evidence of positive impact, these new approaches are more likely to be adopted by other organizations or countries.[101]

16.2 Goals to accomplish

The end goal is creating a "innovation" culture where every employee is thinking about better and different ways of approaching healthcare services and processes simultaneously, within an organization that is willing to invest in change and take risks. Innovation doesn't happen by accident (refer to footnote 89).

16.3 Importance

Why healthcare innovation is important

Innovation is a catalyst that creates value for patients and financial return for stakeholders. When a service or process is not delivered in an optimal or efficient way, there is room for improvement. The realization of incremental or disruptive innovation brings increased tangible value to patients and other stakeholders and expansion of healthcare services to more people.[102]

Key factors that positively influence the innovation implementation process:

- Leadership and management at different tiers that are supportive of and committed to change, including the articulation of a clear and compelling vision
- Early and widespread stakeholder involvement, including staff and service users
- Dedicated and ongoing resources, including funding, staff, infrastructure and time
- Effective communication across the organization
- Ongoing adaptation of the innovation to the local context
- Ongoing monitoring and timely feedback about progress
- Evaluation and demonstration of the (cost-) effectiveness of the innovation being introduced, including assessment of health benefits.

---

99 Rossman, J. 2019. *Think Like Amazon: 50 1/2 Ideas to Become a Digital Leader.* McGraw-Hill Education.

100 World Health Organization Health Innovation Group. WHO. www.who.int/life-course/about/who-health-innovation-group/en/

101 Barnett, J., Vasileiou, K., Djemil, F. et al. 2011. Understanding innovators' experiences of barriers and facilitators in implementation and diffusion of healthcare service innovations: a qualitative study. *BMC Health Services Research.* 11, 342. doi.org/10.1186/1472-6963-11-342.

102 Nolte, E. 2018. How do we ensure that innovation in health service delivery and organization is implemented, sustained and spread? *Policy Brief, Health systems for prosperity and solidarity,* WHO. www.euro.who.int/__data/assets/pdf_file/0004/380731/pb-tallinn-03-eng.pdf

16.4 Best practice

Digital health and gender

Digital health initiatives, including eHealth and mHealth technology-based systems are improving and saving lives in low- and middle-income countries.[103] Furthermore, digital health can positively influence health equity by providing access to trusted information about diseases, treatments, and positive behaviors, as well as personal health records for patients. This is especially true for vulnerable populations and women and girls, in particular. Women face structural and social barriers such as affordability of phones, literacy and digital skills, safety and security, and disapproving families, which may limit their ability to participate in and benefit from digital health initiatives in the same way that men do.[104] Despite these issues, the situation is changing. For example, ownership of mobile phones has expanded rapidly in the Pacific with 95% of women now owning mobile phones.

As digital health becomes more widely adopted and expected by patients and other consumers, it is important to design digital health programs with gender in mind. To positively influence health equity for men and women and girls and boys, incorporating gender perspectives helps to strengthen the impact and coverage of health interventions.[105] Digital health initiatives can deliver a double dividend, using efficient digital technology to target the particular needs of women and girls in the health setting, with greater accuracy. An example is the Liga Inan project in Timor-Leste, which is improving maternal and neonatal care delivery via SMS messaging and direct communications with health providers. When a pregnant woman is registered under the service, she receives twice-weekly health messages, as well as reminders about prenatal checksups. Health providers can also broadcast messages to groups within registered cohorts in the local dialect. Women who have questions can log a request for a call-back from a health professional.

A similar project undertaken and evaluated in Viet Nam recorded a change in gender relations within households, with male partners seeking information on pregnancy and infant development, contrary to traditional gender norms.

Provider-side digital health projects in the Pacific also need to consider the gender disparity within the health workforce. Women are overrepresented in frontline caring roles such as nursing and midwifery professions and underrepresented in decision-making and higher prestige professions, such as physicians.[106] This gender disparity is relevant when designing delivery of digital health services. With training opportunities to enhance digital literacy and to learn data analysis skills for decision-making, female health workers can improve their working relationships and increase their value and status as team members.

Adopting user-centered or human design principles allows for women, as specific stakeholders (users of health services, or providers of health services,) to be separately identified to men. The unique social needs of each group for access to and use of technology can be identified and quantified.[107] Including women in the technology workforce developing digital health projects and in governance structures also helps to make women's voices and experiences heard and visible and brings more diverse perspectives to projects.

For designing of digital health system, best practice gender inclusion involves:

- developing a deep understanding of women as users (healthcare workers or beneficiaries) and the diversity of their situations
- designing the project through conversation, observation and, where possible, co-creation
- formally partnering with women users throughout the project lifecycle to guide their motivation for using technology, their information processing style, technology self-efficacy, attitude toward risk and their technology learning style[108]
- designing, testing and adjusting user interfaces and processes with women until the digital tools meet their needs.

---

103 Sinha, C., Schryer-Roy, A. 2018. Digital health, gender and health equity: invisible imperatives. *Journal of Public Health. October.* www.ncbi.nlm.nih.gov/pmc/articles/PMC6294032/pdf/fdy171.pdf.

104 GSMA. 2020. *The Mobile Gender Gap Report 2020.* www.gsma.com/r/gender-gap/.

105 WHO. n.d. *Gender Policy.* www.who.int/gender/mainstreaming/ENGwhole.pdf.

106 Boniol, M., McIsaac, M., Xu, L., Wuliji, T., Diallo, K. and Campbell, J. 2019. *Gender Equity in the Health Workforce, a study of 104 countries—Health Workforce Working paper 1.* Prepared for the World Health Organization. March. https://apps.who.int/iris/bitstream/handle/10665/311314/WHO-HIS-HWF-Gender-WP1-2019.1-eng.pdf?sequen.

107 ADB. 2018. *Digital Health Impact Framework User Manual, ADB Sustainable Development Working Paper Series* No. 57, November. https://www.adb.org/sites/default/files/publication/465611/sdwp-057-digital-health-impact-framework-manual.pdf

108 Burnett, M. 2020. *Gender-Inclusivity Software Engineering. For the Association for Computing Machinery.* January. YouTube. www.youtube.com/watch?v=tgSn-Ao0VTk.

16.4.1 Develop an innovative culture

> *"Culture is a set of shared values, beliefs and assumptions which strongly influence behaviors, norms and the ways people interact."*[109]

The organization's leadership, either within the Ministry of Health or at a facility level, plays a key role in establishing and nurturing an innovative culture—from being engaged in the organization, promoting creativity, ensuring that reasonable risks and failures are acceptable, and helping navigate the change that comes with implementing innovative ideas.

16.4.2 Facilitate innovation adoption with evidence, partnerships and risk taking

For successful adoption of innovative services or processes several important factors must be in place (refer to footnote 101):

- the ability to demonstrate improved effectiveness of the innovation through "hard" evidence in the form of quantitative data, ideally compared to a target or "gold standard"
- inter-personal and inter-organizational connections through formal and informal partnerships to develop, establish and diffuse the innovations
- the organization must be open to receive new ideas and to address the associated risks that come with innovation
- a flexible budget, even if its small, should be made available to test the innovation.

These key factors for innovation adoption were tested during the COVID-19 pandemic when innovators shared countless solutions to innumerable aspects of the crisis. Evidence-based solutions are the preconditions required for sustainable implementation. There is a need to improve the curation of relevant innovations and knowledge and overcome fragmentations of platform and sources.[110]

16.4.3 Measure the impact of innovation through metrics

In healthcare, it is natural to determine indicators, measure a baseline and monitor the indicators over time. Metrics must be gathered to show change and impact. For others to adopt the innovation, evidence of the positive or negative impacts must be available. Use best practice monitoring and evaluation techniques to measure innovation impact.

16.4.4 Allow for failed experiments

The process of innovation includes creating hypotheses, experimenting, testing, and adjusting (refer to footnote 99). Failure has a different meaning in the context of innovation where experimentation and testing is required to optimize the innovation. Failure is a signal on how a service or process needs to be adjusted. Budget and resources must be allocated to support this deliberate testing and adjusting cycle.

16.4.5 Document a backlog of ideas and a road map

In an organization that values innovation, good ideas will be collected, documented and discussed on a routine basis. With a prioritized list, a road map may be developed. This approach may also be used at a national scale. A set of evaluation criteria should be developed by the appropriate ministry governance group, who will determine the road map and which potential projects will be funded.[111]

16.5 Pitfalls

16.5.1 Policies and bureaucratic barriers

Sometimes organizational barriers or policies stifle innovation. Formal approval processes to test ideas, inflexible security, or confidentiality policies and set rules about staff performing a different job can lead to delays and can kill the initiative outright.[112] Related to this issue is organizational bureaucracy, where people are not specifically accountable and decisions are difficult and slow to make. Innovative organizations need decentralized accountability and decision-making (refer to footnote 99).

[109] Michaelides, D. 2019. Cultivating Innovation Cultures in Healthcare. *Health Management. Vol. 19-Iss 6.* https://healthmanagement.org/c/hospital/issuearticle/cultivating-innovation-cultures-in-healthcare.

[110] Merten, M., Roth, S., Allaudin, F.S. 2020. *Public Health Innovations for COVID-19: Finding, Trusting, and Scaling Innovation.* https://www.adb.org/sites/default/files/publication/648131/sdwp-70-public-health-inovations-covid-19.pdf.

[111] Loria, K. n.d. *3 Ways to Make Healthcare More Innovative, Managed Health Executive.* www.managedhealthcareexecutive.com/view/3-ways-make-healthcare-more-innovative.

[112] Australian Government. n.d. *Barriers to innovation in the APS.* www.apsc.gov.au/4-barriers-innovation-aps.

16.5.2 Adoption of innovations without proven efficacy

Implementing the newest technology innovation that promises to improve the quality of care or reduce costs should be backed up by evidence and data. It is easy to assume that better data collection tools, more up-to-date devices, or easier access to information will ultimately lead to better patient outcomes. These assumptions need to be tested, together with updates to process and training and support for the users of the new technology.[113] For example, mobile phone technology has transformed the lives of people in the Pacific and is widely used for health and educational purposes.[114] The assumption is that using mobile technology will increase positive patient outcomes; however, the exact context must be piloted and the effectiveness measured.

16.5.3 Lack of strong leadership willing to take calculated risks

Healthcare, as an industry, is risk averse, with a focus on avoiding errors and maintaining system stability, rather than taking risks and making advancements. Traditional healthcare leaders are careful, practical planners who try to keep as many stakeholders as happy as possible.[115] Patients expect innovative approaches to the healthcare delivered to them, whether access to better data collection and use through electronic health records, access to their healthcare data through portals, or new medical devices. Leaders must be able to manage risk and develop or hire staff with the skills and knowledge for successful experimentation and optimization of services and processes.

16.6 Quick tip

Establish an innovation team or task force within a country, region, facility, or organization that collects ideas and works with teams to implement innovations.

16.7 Practice spotlight

Delivery of vaccines by drones in Vanuatu

In December 2018, the Vanuatu Ministry of Health, with the support of UNICEF, the Australian Government's Department of Foreign Affairs and Trade, and the Global Fund, successfully delivered vaccines by drones across rugged, mountainous terrain on the remote islands of Epi and the Shepherds Islands, Erromango, and Pentecost.

In Vanuatu, one in five children are not immunized, partly because transporting vaccines is so difficult and costly. Healthcare workers have to carry vaccines in iceboxes across difficult terrain.

Two commercial drone operators, Swoop Aero and WingCopter, were selected to conduct trials with test payloads. The first flight carrying vaccines in Styrofoam boxes with icepacks and a thermometer was received by a registered nurse who administered vaccines to 13 children and 5 pregnant women. What would have taken hours to deliver by boat and on foot, took 25 minutes by drone.

This innovative program is promising and could prove to be sustainable if adequate scale is reached. Compared to sending boats and people, drones are more economical. The commercial drone operators also cover the risk if a payload does not reach its destination.

A key success factor of the program was the introduction of the concept to villagers by local nurses and community leaders, explaining how the drones work and how the program can help keep children healthy. An exciting outcome of this initiative is that vaccines can be sent on demand, better matching the needs of a community.

113 Dixon-Woods M., Amalberti R., Goodman S., Bergmans, B. and Glasziou, P. 2011. Problems and promises of innovation: why healthcare needs to rethink its love/hate relationship with the new. *British Medical Journal of Quality & Safety, 20:i47-i51.* https://qualitysafety.bmj.com/content/20/Suppl_1/i47.

114 GSMA. 2019. *The Mobile Economy Pacific Islands.* www.gsma.com/mobileeconomy/pacific-islands/.

115 Hart, R.I. 2016. The need for innovative leadership in healthcare'. *Becker's Hospital Review, Leadership & Management. December.* www.beckershospitalreview.com/hospital-management-administration/the-need-for-innovative-leadership-in-healthcare.html.

"In remote settings like Vanuatu, safely getting vaccines and other essential medical supplies to children presents a unique set of challenges," said Sheldon Yett, UNICEF Pacific Representative. "We are proud to support the Government of Vanuatu in exploring new ways to get vaccines safely where they need to go, when they need to go."

See these videos of these trials at:

UNICEF: www.youtube.com/watch?v=jdvbcv6_TcE

Aljazeera: www.youtube.com/watch?v=RXyspnAI9-0

16.8 Resources and references

Reference: Digital Health Innovation: A Toolkit to Navigate From Concept to Clinical Testing

Reference: Australian Government: Public Sector Innovation Network This network attracts Australian public servants and innovation leaders from around the world. The site offers free membership along with an active, weekly newsletter. It also provides a set of free tools that may be useful for your digital health projects.

Reference: Working innovatively: A toolkit to support the use of innovative technology in practice

Reference: Creating an innovation center of excellence

Reference: The 7 Things Every Innovation Center Should Have

Reference: Free software tool the help guide and manage the collection, evaluation and prioritization of ideas.

Reference: Public Health Innovations for COVID-19: Findings, Trusting and Scaling Innovation

Registered nurse, Miriam Nampil, receives the first vaccine delivery from the Swoop Aero drone in Vanuatu in 2018 (photo by UNICEF).

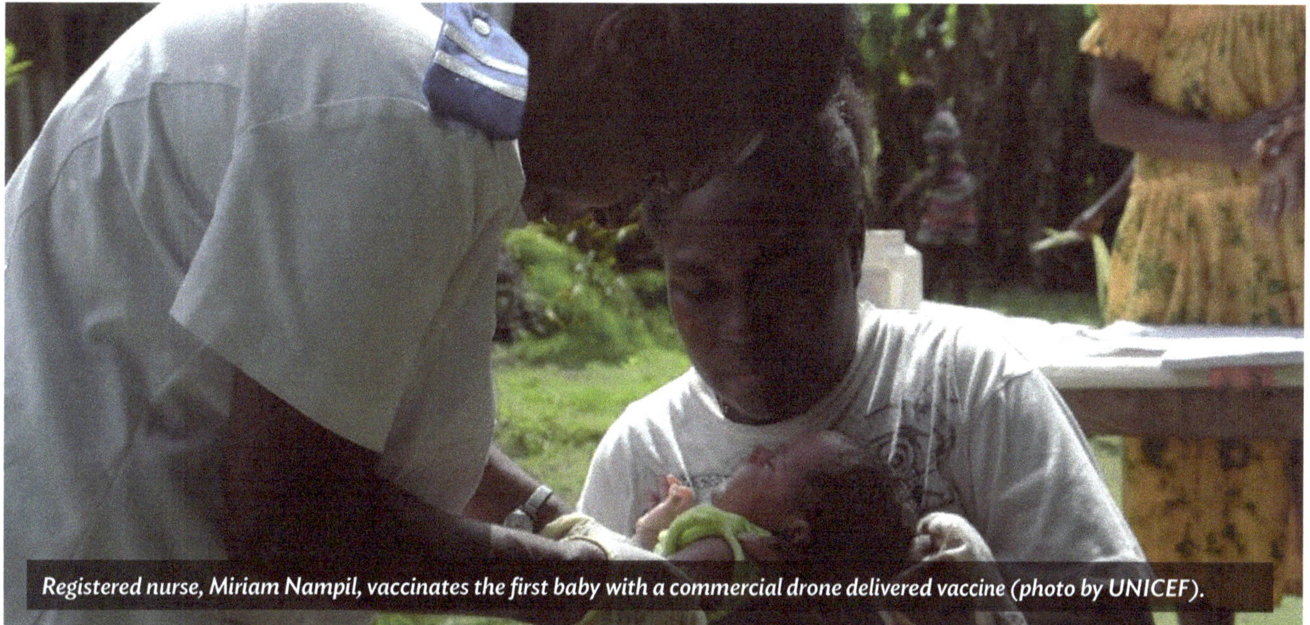

Registered nurse, Miriam Nampil, vaccinates the first baby with a commercial drone delivered vaccine (photo by UNICEF).

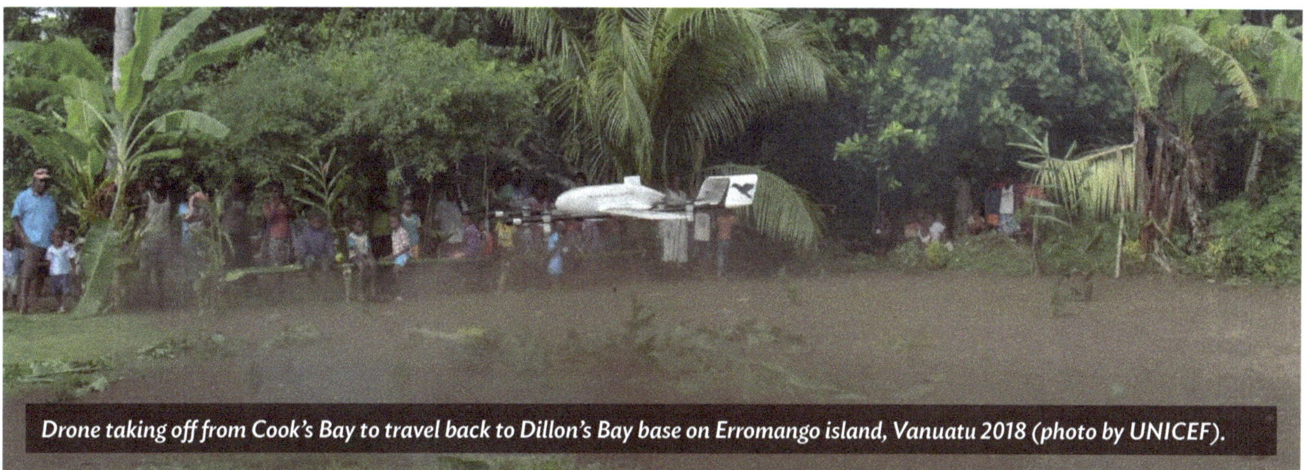

Drone taking off from Cook's Bay to travel back to Dillon's Bay base on Erromango island, Vanuatu 2018 (photo by UNICEF).

This guide includes experiences from Pacific island countries that have already invested in digital health, and brings together a collection of references, practical tools, and resources to guide all stages of digital health implementation and use (photo by ADB).

REFERENCES

ADB. 2018. *Digital Health Impact Framework User Manual,* ADB Sustainable Development Working Paper Series No. 57, November. www.adb.org/sites/default/files/publication/465611/sdwp-057-digital-health-impact-framework-manual.pdf.

ADB. 2018. *Guidance for Investing in Digital Health,* May. www.adb.org/publications/guidance-investing-digital-health.

ADB. 2018. *Unique Health Identifier Assessment Tool Kit.* May. https://www.adb.org/documents/unique-health-identifier-assessment-toolkit.

ADB and Asian eHealth Information Network. 2018. *Digital Health Terminology Guide.* March. http://sil-asia.org/digital-health-terminology-guide/.

Aidinyantz, N. 2017. *How to Run a Phishing Simulation Test: An Example from GlobalSign. GlobalSign.* https://www.globalsign.com/en/blog/how-to-run-a-simulated-phishing-test.

American Health Information Management Association. 2014. *Equipping the Future eHealth Workforce through Global Curriculum Standards. Slide deck. U.S. Department of Commerce—International Trade Association Market Development Cooperator Program award #IT13MAS1120001.* www.ahima.org/~/media/AHIMA/Files/AHIMA-and-Our-Work/AHIMADOCMDCPOverviewcompressed.ashx.

Ammenwerth, E., Gräber, S., Herrmann G., Bürkled, T., König., J. 2003. Evaluation of health information systems—problems and challenges. *International Journal of Medical Informatics July.*

Andriotis, N. 2017. *The Workforce Development Strategy Tips to Make Your Staff Stand Out! eFront.* https://bit.ly/2TCqOZS.

Australian Government. n.d. *Barriers to innovation in the APS.* www.apsc.gov.au/4-barriers-innovation-aps.

Australian Government. 2013. Cabinet Implementation Unit Toolkit. Governance, Department of the Prime Minister and Cabinet. June. www.pmc.gov.au/sites/default/files/files/pmc/implementation-toolkit-2-governance.pdf.

Barnett, J., Vasileiou, K., Djemil, F. et al. 2011. Understanding innovators' experiences of barriers and facilitators in implementation and diffusion of healthcare service innovations: a qualitative study. *BMC Health Services Research. 11, 342.* doi.org/10.1186/1472-6963-11-342.

Bass, L., Clements, P. Kazman, R. and Wesley, A. 2003. *Software Architecture in Practice. Second edition.*

Beck, E.J. et. al. 2018. Developing and implementing national health identifiers in resource limited countries: why, what, who, when and how? *Global Health Action,* Vol 11.

Berryman, R., Yost, N., Dunn, N., and Edwards, C. 2013. *Data Interoperability and Information Security in Healthcare. Transactions of the International Conference on Health Information Technology Advancement,* 26 October. https://scholarworks.wmich.edu/ichita_transactions/26.

BMC Blogs. 2019. SaaS vs PaaS vs IaaS: What's The Difference and How To Choose. June. www.bmc.com/blogs/saas-vs-paas-vs-iaas-whats-the-difference-and-how-to-choose/.

Boniol, M., McIsaac, M., Xu, L., Wuliji, T., Diallo, K. and Campbell, J. 2019. *Gender Equity in the Health Workforce, a study of 104 countries—Health Workforce Working paper 1.* Prepared for the World Health Organization. March. https://apps.who.int/iris/bitstream/handle/10665/311314/WHO-HIS-HWF-Gender-WP1-2019.1-eng.pdf?sequen.

Brunner M., McGregor, D., Keep M., et al. 2018. An eHealth Capabilities Framework for Graduates and Health Professionals: Mixed-Methods Study. *Journal of Medical Internet Research, 20(5):e10229.* May. doi:10.2196/10229.

Burling-Phillips, L. 2013. *Patient Portals, Part 1: First Steps for Your Practice, American Academy of Ophthalmology.* December. www.aao.org/eyenet/article/patient-portals-part-1-first-steps-your-practice-2.

Burling-Phillips, L. 2014. *Patient Portals, Part 2: What Features Do You Need? American Academy of Ophthalmology,* January, www.aao.org/eyenet/article/patient-portals-part-2-what-features-do-you-need.

Burnett, M. 2020. *Gender-Inclusivity Software Engineering. For the Association for Computing Machinery. January. YouTube.* www.youtube.com/watch?v=tgSn-AoOVTk.

Canada Health Infoway. 2013. A Framework and Toolkit for Managing eHealth Change: People and Processes. March. https://bit.ly/2ZobwKn.

Capacity Project. n.d. *HRH Action Framework.* www.capacityproject.org/framework/hr-management-systems/

Carroll, L.N., Au, A.P., Detwiler, L.T., Fu, T., Painter, I.S., and Abernethy, N.F. 2014. Visualization and analytics tools for infectious disease epidemiology: A systematic review'. *Journal of Biomedical Informatics.* 51. pp. 287–298.

Center for Disease Control. 2015. *Vaccine Storage and Handling Toolkit.* April. https://www.cdc.gov/vaccines/hcp/admin/storage/toolkit/storage-handling-toolkit.pdf.

Cisco. n.d. *What is a Data Center?* www.cisco.com/c/en/us/solutions/data-center-virtualization/what-is-a-data-center.html.

Cisco. 2019. *Reaching 650 Million: How Digital Technology is Key to Achieving Universal Health Coverage in ASEAN.* www.cisco.com/c/dam/global/en_sg/assets/pdfs/healthcare.pdf.

Conceição Granja, C. Janssen, W., Johansen, M.A. 2018. 'Factors Determining the Success and Failure of eHealth Interventions: Systematic Review of the Literature', Journal of Medical Internet Research. May. www.ncbi.nlm.nih.gov/pmc/articles/PMC5954232/.

Cometto, G., Buchan, J., Dussault, G. 2020. Developing the health workforce for universal health coverage. *Bulletin of the World Health Organization.* www.ncbi.nlm.nih.gov/pmc/articles/PMC6986219/.

Dashlane. 2020. How to run an effective phishing test at work. 7 March. https://blog.dashlane.com/phishing-test/

Data Foundry. 2019. *Estimating Data Center Cost of Ownership: 5 Hidden Costs.* August. www.datafoundry.com/blog/estimating-data-center-cost-ownership-5-hidden-costs.

De Bakker, K., Boonstra, A., and Wortmann, H. (2010). 'Does risk management contribute to IT project success? A meta-analysis of empirical evidence', *International Journal of Project Management, University of Groningen, The Netherlands.*

Dendere, R., Slade, C., Burton-Jones, A., Sullivan, C., Staib, A., & Janda, M. 2019. *Patient Portals Facilitating Engagement With Inpatient Electronic Medical Records: A Systematic Review. Journal of Medical Internet Research. 21(4). e12779.* https://doi.org/10.2196/12779

Dixon-Woods M., Amalberti R., Goodman S., Bergmans, B. and Glasziou, P. 2011. *Problems and promises of innovation: why healthcare needs to rethink its love/hate relationship with the new. British Medical Journal of Quality & Safety, 20:i47-i51.* https://qualitysafety.bmj.com/content/20/Suppl_1/i47.

Drury, P., Roth, S., Jones, T., Stahl, M., and Medeiros, D. 2018. *Guidance for investing in digital health. ADB. May. No. 52.* www.adb.org/sites/default/files/publication/424311/sdwp-052-guidance-investing-digital-health.pdf.

Fanta, G.B., Pretorius, I., and Erasmus, L. 2015. An evaluation of ehealth systems implementation frameworks for sustainability in resource constrained environments: a literature review. *International Association for Management of Technology, 2015 Conference Proceedings.*

Gersh, L. 2013. *'The Velocity of Obsolescence'. Forbes.com.* July. www.forbes.com/sites/lewisgersh/2013/07/29/the-velocity-of-obsolescence/#3256f72a6596.

Government of Papua New Guinea. 2017. *The National eHealth Strategy 2017–2027.*

Granja, C., Janssen, W., Johansen, M. A. 2018. Factors Determining the Success and Failure of eHealth Interventions: Systematic Review of the Literature. *Journal of Medical Internet Research.* May. 20(5): e10235. https://www.ncbi.nlm.nih.gov/pmc/articles/PMC5954232/.

Green, J. 2019. How much EHR costs and how to set your budget. *EHR in Practice,* March.

GSMA. 2019. *The Mobile Economy Pacific Islands.* www.gsma.com/mobileeconomy/pacific-islands/.

GSMA. 2019. *The State of Mobile Internet Connectivity.* www.gsma.com/mobilefordevelopment/wp-content/uploads/2019/07/GSMA-State-of-Mobile-Internet-Connectivity-Report-2019.pdf.

GSMA. 2020. *The Mobile Gender Gap Report 2020.* www.gsma.com/r/gender-gap/.

Hanby, J. 2016. *Software Maintenance: Understanding and Estimating Costs.* Lookfar blog. Oct. http://blog.lookfar.com/blog/2016/10/21/software-maintenance-understanding-and-estimating-costs/.

Hardee, K., 2008. *Data Quality Audit Tool, Guidelines for Implementation,* MEASURE Evaluation Project. MS-08-29 September.

Harin, E. 2020. A complete guide to RACI/RASCI charts. https://www.girlsguidetopm.com/a-complete-guide-to-raci-rasci-charts/.

Hart, R. I. 2016. The need for innovative leadership in healthcare'. *Becker's Hospital Review, Leadership & Management.* December. www.beckershospitalreview.com/hospital-management-administration/the-need-for-innovative-leadership-in-healthcare.html.

Healthcare Information and Management Systems Society, Inc. (HIMSS). n.d. Interoperability in Healthcare. www.himss.org/resources/interoperability-healthcare.

HealthIT.gov. n.d. *What is a patient portal?* www.healthit.gov/faq/what-patient-portal.

Huang, F., Blaschke, S., Lucas, H., 2017. Beyond pilotitis: taking digital health interventions to the national level in China and Uganda, *Globalization and Health.* https://globalizationandhealth.biomedcentral.com/articles/10.1186/s12992-017-0275-z.

Irizarry, T., DeVito Dabbs, A., & Curran, C. R. 2015. Patient Portals and Patient Engagement: A State of the Science Review. *Journal of Medical Internet Research. 17(6). e148.* https://doi.org/10.2196/jmir.4255.

Jarocki, T. 2013. *PMI Project Management versus Change Management: Similarities, Overlaps and Differences, Journal of Change Management Community of Practice, ProjectManagement.com. Webinar.* June www.projectmanagement.com/videos/286316/Project-Management-vs-Change-Management.

Khoja, S., et.al. 2007. e-Health Readiness Assessment Tools for Healthcare Institutions in Developing Countries. *Telemedicine Journal and e-Health.* September.

Kiberu, V., Mars, M., Scott, R., 2019. *Development of an evidence-based e-health readiness assessment framework for Uganda. Health Information Management Journal.* April.

Kitskoo 2019. *e-Government Assessment & Recommendation for The Cook Islands,* April.

Kitskoo. 2019. *Government of the Cook Islands eGovernment Assessment & Recommendation presentation,* May.

Krishnamurthy, R. 2015. Developing a National eHealth Strategy. *World Health Organization Headquarters Ministry of Public Health Conference on eHealth Strategy.* Bangkok, Thailand. 18 March.

Loria, K. n.d. *3 Ways to Make Healthcare More Innovative, Managed Health Executive.* www.managedhealthcareexecutive.com/view/3-ways-make-healthcare-more-innovative.

Marcelo, A., Medeiros, D., Ramesh, K., Roth, S., and Wyatt, P. 2018. *Transforming Health Systems Through Good Digital Health Governance. ADB.* February. https://www.adb.org/sites/default/files/publication/401976/sdwp-051-transforming-health-systems.pdf.

Marvel, F.A., Wang, J., Martin. S.S. 2018. Digital Health Innovation: A Toolkit to Navigate From Concept to Clinical Testing. *JMIR Cardio* 2(1).

Matheson, D., Douglas, M., Bhattacharya, S., 2017. *Independent Review of the PNG NHIS for Rural Primary Health Services Delivery. Manila: ADB.*

Mauco, L., Scott, R., and Mars, M., 2020. *Validation of an e-health readiness assessment framework for developing countries. BMC Health Services Research—under review,* March.

MEASURE Evaluation Project 2011. Tools for Data Demand and Use in the Health Sector—Framework for Linking Data with Action. *Measure Evaluation Manual.* ms-11-46b, April. www.measureevaluation.org/resources/publications/ms-11-46-b.

MEASURE Evaluation. 2019. *Health Information Systems Interoperability Maturity Toolkit: Users' Guide Version 1.0.* January. www.measureevaluation.org/resources/publications/tl-17-03a. www.measureevaluation.org/resources/publications/ms-11-46-b.

Menachemi, N. and Collum, T. 2011. Benefits and drawbacks of electronic health record systems. *Risk Management and Healthcare Policy.* 2011.

Merten, M., Roth, S., Allaudin, F.S. 2020. *Public Health Innovations for COVID-19: Finding, Trusting, and Scaling Innovation.* https://www.adb.org/sites/default/files/publication/648131/sdwp-70-public-health-inovations-covid-19.pdf.

Michaelides, D. 2019. *Cultivating Innovation Cultures in Healthcare. Health Management. Vol. 19-Iss 6.* https://healthmanagement.org/c/hospital/issuearticle/cultivating-innovation-cultures-in-healthcare.

Miller, D. P., Jr, Latulipe, C., Melius, K. A., Quandt, S. A., & Arcury, T. A. 2016. Primary Care Providers' Views of Patient Portals: Interview Study of Perceived Benefits and Consequences. *Journal of Medical Internet Research, 18(1), e8.* https://doi.org/10.2196/jmir.4953.

Ministry of Health. *Kenya National eHealth Policy 2016–2030. p. 24.* https://health.eac.int/publications/kenya-national-ehealth-policy-2016-2030.

Munoz-Cornejo, G., Seaman, C.B., and Koru, G. 2009. An Empirical Investigation into the Adoption of Open Source Software in Hospitals. *International Journal of Healthcare Information Systems and Informatics. January.* www.researchgate.net/publication/220168739_An_Empirical_Investigation_into_the_Adoption_of_Open_Source_Software_in_Hospitals.

Nieves, R. 2018. '3 tips on managing change in a hospital's digital transformation'. Elsevier Connect, February. https://www.elsevier.com/connect/3-tips-on-managing-change-in-a-hospitals-digital-transformation.

Nolte, E. 2018. How do we ensure that innovation in health service delivery and organization is implemented, sustained and spread? *Policy Brief, Health systems for prosperity and solidarity,* WHO. www.euro.who.int/__data/assets/pdf_file/0004/380731/pb-tallinn-03-eng.pdf

Ogoe, H.A., Asamani, J.A., Hochheiser, H., Douglas, G.P. 2018. Assessing Ghana's eHealth workforce: implications for planning and training. *Human Resources for Health. November.* https://bit.ly/2LZbRN6.

Orlova, A., Bourquard, K., and Parisot, C. 2017. Understanding User Needs for Interoperability: Standards for Business Cases in eHealth, *Journal of AHIMA 88. No.7 (July): 34–37.*

Papua new Guinea Ministry of Health. 2011. *National Health Plan 2011–2020.* https://www.health.gov.pg/subindex.php?acts=1.

Project Management Institute. 2017. *A guide to the project management body of knowledge* (PMBOK GUIDE). Sixth edition.

Ritz, D. 2016. Caring for #EVERYCHILD. Video 2 of 3. https://vimeo.com/156650602.

Rossman, J. 2019. *Think Like Amazon: 50 1/2 Ideas to Become a Digital Leader.* McGraw-Hill Education.

Roth, S., Parry, J., and Thit, W.M. 2018. *Digital Health Convergence Meeting Tool Kit.* November. https://www.adb.org/publications/digital-health-convergence-meeting-tool-kit.

Rouse, M. 2007. *Lights-out management (LOM). SearchDataCenter.* https://searchdatacenter.techtarget.com/definition/lights-out-management.

Russo, A.K., Dussault, G. et al. 2010. Costing the scaling-up of human resources for health: lessons from Mozambique and Guinea Bissau. *Human Resources for Health.* 8, 14. https://doi.org/10.1186/1478-4491-8-14.

Scott, R.E. and Mars, M. 2013. Principles and Framework for eHealth Strategy Development. Journal of Medical Internet Research. Vol. 15, No 7. www.jmir.org/2013/7/e155/.

Sinha, C., Schryer-Roy, A. 2018. Digital health, gender and health equity: invisible imperatives. *Journal of Public Health.* October. www.ncbi.nlm.nih.gov/pmc/articles/PMC6294032/pdf/fdy171.pdf.

Siwicki, B. 2020. *Privacy & security perspectives: Interoperability, prospects for HIPAA refresh, more. Healthcare IT News.* June.

Spigel, L., Wambugu, S., and Villella, C. 2018. mHealth Data Security, Privacy, and Confidentiality: Guidelines for Program Implementers and Policymakers, MEASURE Evaluation, January.

Stahl, M., Roth, S. Thorell, L., and Parry, J. 2016. On the road to universal health coverage: Every person matters, *ADB Briefs*. https://www.adb.org/sites/default/files/publication/183512/uhc-every-person-matters.pdf.

Sulaiman, R., Sharma, D., Ma, W., and Tran, D. 2008. *A Security Architecture for e-Health Services. International Conference on Advanced Communication Technology.* March 2008. https://www.researchgate.net/publication/4325306_A_Security_Architecture_for_e-Health_Services.Tyrrell,

Tolley, H. Snowdon, W., Wate, J., Durand, A.M., Vivili, P., McCool1, J., Novotny, R., Dewes, O., Hoy, D., Bell, C., Richards, N., and Swinburn, B. 2016. Monitoring and accountability for the Pacific response to the non-communicable diseases crisis. *BMC Public Health*. 16:958, DOI 10.1186/s12889-016-3614-8. www.ncbi.nlm.nih.gov/pmc/articles/PMC5018177/pdf/12889_2016_Article_3614.pdf.

UNAIDS. 2014. *Considerations and guidance for countries adopting national health identifiers. Joint United Nations Programme on HIV/AIDS.*

US Department of Health and Human Services, (n.d.) *Health Information privacy, Guidance Regarding Methods for De-identification of Protected Health Information in Accordance with the Health Insurance Portability and Accountability Act (HIPAA) Privacy Rule.* www.hhs.gov/hipaa/for-professionals/privacy/special-topics/de-identification/index.html#protected.

Wilson, K., Gertz, B., Arenth, B. and Salisbury N. 2014. *The journey to scale: Moving together past digital health pilots. Seattle: PATH. World Health Organization. 2008. Assessing the National Health Information System, An Assessment Tool.* Version 4.00. Health Metrics Network.

World Health Organization. n.d. *Gender Policy.* www.who.int/gender/mainstreaming/ENGwhole.pdf.

World Health Organization. 2008. *Toolkit on monitoring health systems strengthening, Health Information Systems,* June.

World Health Organization. 2008. *Financing and economic aspects of health workforce scale-up and improvement: framework paper: Alliance financing task force.* October. www.who.int/workforcealliance/knowledge/publications/taskforces/frameworkpaper.pdf.

World Health Organization. 2012. National eHealth Strategy Toolkit. www.itu.int/dms_pub/itu-d/opb/str/D-STR-E_HEALTH.05-2012-PDF-E.pdf.

World Health Organization. 2012. 'The bigger picture for e-health', *Bulletin of the World Health Organization*, Volume 90, Number 5, May, pp. 321–40.

World Health Organization. 2015. *MAPS Toolkit mHealth Assessment and Planning for Scale.* https://apps.who.int/iris/bitstream/handle/10665/185238/9789241509510_eng.pdf?sequence=1.

World Health Organization. 2017. Health information systems in the Pacific—at a glance 2016. Regional Office for the Western Pacific. Manila, Philippines. https://apps.who.int/iris/rest/bitstreams/1147902/retrieve.

World Health Organization. 2017. *Data Quality Review,* Modules 1–3. World Health Organization Health Innovation Group. World Health Organization. www.who.int/life-course/about/who-health-innovation-group/en/.

World Health Organization. 2020. *Digital implementation Investment Guide (DIIG): Integrating Digital Interventions into health programmes.* https://www.who.int/publications/i/item/9789240010567.

World Health Organization and International Telecommunications Union TU. 2012. National eHealth Strategy Toolkit. www.itu.int/dms_pub/itu-d/opb/str/D-STR-E_HEALTH.05-2012-PDF-E.pdf.

World Population Review. n.d. Papua New Guinea Population. https://worldpopulationreview.com/countries/papua-new-guinea-population.

Wu, L. 2016. *Recommendations for a Global Framework to Support Health Information Exchange in Low- and Middle-Income Countries. Regenstrief Institute.* November.

www.ingramcontent.com/pod-product-compliance
Lightning Source LLC
Chambersburg PA
CBHW050047220326
41599CB00045B/7320
9789292628550

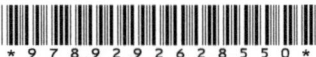